"Though no one can go back and make a brand new start, anyone can start from now and make a brand new ending." —Carl Bard

Be your own Hero

X

Mindset Mojo

The Art of feeling better

Jane Bellis

"How to free your mind of anxiety and stress & Find your Mojo"

For Pam

Contents

Foreword

It's been a funny old journey that's led me to this point in time, sitting here at my laptop pouring out my heart and soul into a manuscript that, if five years ago you had told me I would be writing, I would have laughed at.

Life deals us a strange hand sometimes – and for me that is the big reveal, and something that I aim to uncover through the pages of this book.

Are we simply bystanders travelling through a period in time, being affected by our environment, surroundings and the 'things' that happen to us? Do we really have no control other than to observe and react? For the first 35 years of my life I would have said yes, and found comfort in the fact that things 'weren't my fault' and I 'had no choice' – but something stirred and shifted in me sometime during 2012 (as it did for a lot of people I later found out)

This 'shift' of consciousness led to me giving up my career in beauty and fashion, selling my salons, travelling to Peru to visit Machu Pichu, having a near death experience (or two), and returning to embark on what has become an amazing decade of discovery, challenges, learning and re-learning whilst I found my Tribe and started to re-write the ending to my story in a way that I would never had thought possible with my own limiting beliefs.

Developing Mindset Mojo as a coaching and development programme had been an absolute joy, and really has been food for my soul, not to mention fertilizer for my brain!

In this book I would like to share some of the learning that I discovered through some amazing, inspirational teachers from around the world, and the practical self-help tools and techniques that form my practical and digital Mindset Mojo courses and workshops.

The material in this book is based on my own personal experience, opinion, and research, and is not intended to replace medical or other professional advice, treatment or support. I encourage you to explore all avenues and discover your own personal truth

Introduction

We are living in a time where we are expected to deal with physical, mental and emotional stress on a daily basis, without having any knowledge, training or even clues as to how we are supposed to cope. As fragile human beings we have inbuilt mechanisms to help us to survive as a species, including our emotional attachments to help with procreation and family bonds, our sympathetic nervous system response to help us to dodge predators, and an extremely complex supercomputer between our ears that has evolved a great deal over the past few hundred years, but unfortunately doesn't come with a user guide or instruction manual.

We are born with factory settings programmed in through years of DNA code transference from generation to generation, which is geared to give us the best possible chance of surviving this crazy thing called life, evolving that little bit more in order to keep the system moving, and pass the baton on to the next wave of 'Mini Me's. One of the main problems as I can see it, is that not only are we not taught or encouraged to customize those settings for optimum user experience, we are in fact vehemently DISCOURAGED from thinking, feeling and behaving anything other than what society dictates through an endless web of social conditioning through mainstream media, corporate and government narratives. We are not taught or shown that the unique recipes that make us who we are should be discovered, embraced and nurtured in order for us to live our true purpose and our best lives. We are taught to be more concerned with what we are PERCEIVED to be than who we really are. This is a very sad and dangerous game that we find ourselves in, and in my opinion is the root cause of the Mental Health crisis that we are slap bang in the middle of right now.

During my exploration of mental health, neuroscience, psychology and human behaviour, I have discovered that although we have these universal factory settings, there is a blueprint deep inside our DNA just waiting to be decoded. The very fabric of what makes you 'you' – that super special alchemic mix of ingredients that is totally unique to you. The tragedy is that so few people get to reach their true potential and express their true selves, due to a society programmed to conformity, fear, intolerance, power and control.

Have you ever wondered what it would be like if you could free yourself from the chains of expectation? If you didn't have to worry about what other people thought? If 'fitting in' and being accepted wasn't an issue, or that you could never ever let anybody down or fail at anything because everything you do is just perfect for you, even if not by other people's standards and expectations? How would that feel, to live in a world where your deepest, darkest desires, wants needs and goals that stay hidden in the shadows due to fear of ridicule, could shimmer to the surface and illuminate your life?

During the course of this book we will delve deeper into our mind-body connection, look at our thoughts, emotions, values, expectations and behaviours, and take a leap into the unknown to discover neuroplasticity, brain reprogramming, and our connection with our higher, subconscious selves, learning how to shift those old beliefs and negative behaviour patterns that have been holding us back for so long.

Buckle up buttercup .... You're in for an internal adventure!

Chapter 1: Who are you?!

"Society creates a context where you are encouraged to be more concerned about who you are perceived to be than who you really are.
Socially constructed conformity undermines diversity and individuality, but it does not have to be this way. You can create a different story. You need to look at YOUR inner story – and be careful not to hand authorship over to others" – Dr Tim O'Brien

This has to be one of my all-time favourite quotes since I saw Dr Tim O'Brien speak at a Wellbeing conference in Cardiff. It really stuck with me as although Tim's background as a professor of Psychology & Human development was in Sports, notably his role as Arsenal's 'mind' guy, and the speaking gig he was at was around stress management and wellbeing in the Education sector – everything that he had to say (and in particular this quote which I discovered later on in his book) related to my own life, not least my journey through the fashion industry from the mid 90's to present day.

Everywhere I look, whether the communities I work with, my salon clients when I still worked in the beauty industry, my family, friends or passing acquaintances – everybody seemed to be playing a part. One that they had convinced themselves was necessary in order to please others, avoid ridicule, and simply 'fit in', and this has bothered me for as long as I can remember, to the point that I have now given up my entire career to embark on another.

I have now dedicated my life to completely retraining to learn about human psychology and behaviour, neuroscience and the mind-body connection – hunting high and low for any snippets of information I could find that might shed some light onto this phenomenon, which has caused 99% of the people that I have come into contact with (whether they admit it at first or not!) to sacrifice without question their own happiness, wants, needs, desires and gifts, and forego their true life path which has been encoded into their very DNA .... So that they can be accepted into a society that does its very best to batter them down at every turn.

My aim, through Mindset Mojo courses, coaching and indeed this very book, is to shine some light on the shadows and expose some of the fundamental flaws within today's society – the lack of education when it comes to being human. If only we were taught from an early age the connection between mind and body, the affect that our experiences, interactions and relationships have on our emotional, chemical and biological responses, and the resulting behaviour patterns that are programmed in to be repeated again and again throughout our lives. If only we were made aware that feelings, both good and bad were not the enemy, but actually our internal barometers, guiding us through life and encouraging us to use our judgement and discernment as to what is right for us.

Surely if we were shown that we have the constant power to be able to make choices or excuses and that these decisions lie firmly at our feet, we would be able to see through the social constructs to what really mattered. If only we were encouraged to discover our creative power, to daydream, think big and turn inwards, learning to work with our innate 'instincts' and follow that gut feeling to access our true power and our own unique path to happiness and fulfillment.

If we were empowered to let our true lights shine brightly without fear of ridicule, intolerance or hatred, and allowed to pass that light on, we could light the touch paper for other beautiful souls to reach their true potential too.

Well now is your chance. The pages of this book provide a safe environment for you to discover, analyse, consider, build, and create profound change in your life.

Please note here that this book is not a substitute for medical treatment or professional guidance, nor is it intended to challenge religious, spiritual, or scientific beliefs.

It is simply an experiential guide, detailing my journey so far into the unknown. The internal and external steps that I have taken to elevate my consciousness to create profound changes in my own, and others lives – and hey, if it's working for myself and those around me, why wouldn't I want to share it with the world!

My advice to you, is to read this book with an open mind. Leave your preconceptions, judgements, and basic assumptions on life at the door, and delve in with eyes, minds and hearts wide open. If the contents resonate with you in some way, then please join me and engage in some of the exercises laid out for you.

Above all, I have written this book from the heart. My ultimate truth, laid bare with all of the honesty, integrity, compassion, love and gratitude I have within me.

Faking it

Before we go any further in to discovering the real you, let me just shed a little light on a long-forgotten thing called 'Real Life'.

For my entire adult life, and a 25 year career in the fashion, beauty & media industries, I have been around bulls**t – a total 360 degree 'Matrix blue pill' style alternative reality. From models living off half an apple and a line of cocaine a day to stay in that bizarre version of production line perfection, to the clients that came into my salon with cripplingly low self-esteem because they didn't look anything like the aforementioned 'beautiful people' – yet engineered their social media highlights with filters and stories that suggested anything but their reality.

Moving on to global fashion events, with the bright lights and intoxicating buzz of NYC during fashion week, with the paparazzi, magazine covers, interviews and voxpops – all pointing towards a never ending frenzy of gorgeousness and desirability from the horrendously over priced garments to the miracle beauty cures, all designed to prey on our vulnerabilities and perceived inadequacies in order to turn a profit. The rich get richer and the rest of us end up in therapy.

No sign of the blood, sweat and tears that go in to planning, producing and covering such events, or the burnout, exhaustion, addiction and physical & psychological trauma that goes hand in perfect hand with the industry.

What about the blood, sweat and tears that go into the production of the immaculate fashion garments and accessories, the collateral damage of countless children working ridiculous hours in factories, or the animals suffering unspeakable pain and trauma just so we can have our favourite beauty hack?

Of course, sometimes we get a glimmer of reality, before we shut it down because it spoils the illusion that we've eaten up for our whole lives – it's so much easier to keep on scrolling and find something else mind numbing and easy to digest, perhaps a picture of someone's perfect dinner, or a cute animal meme to distract us and make us feel temporarily better.

We are living in a snap chatting, tiktokking, facebooking, teeth whitening, butt lifting, lip plumping, wrinkle reducing, brain numbing, body abusing, happiness reducing society which seems to be getting worse and worse by the day. So where do we go from here? How do we un-programme these super strong beliefs about ourselves and the world around us that the media have spent so much time, effort and money constructing?

We strip it all back. We step out of our fear and into our light.

Change is a difficult thing for anyone to manage – but when you can learn to embrace positive change it will rewrite the end to your story, and you have full control of the pen.

(seriously, you need to go get a pen, we have work to do my friend!)

So, what are we afraid of? Why do we get that niggling feeling when someone asks us to be honest about ourselves? Why does our sympathetic nervous system activate a stress response when we're posed with the question 'what are you really good at' or 'what's your secret desire?'
We're going to start looking in some detail in the next chapter about the psychology & physiology behind it all, but for now we will just touch on the social reasons behind our inability to admit what we really want, take compliments, or celebrate the things that we are really epic at.

Rewinding back to our evolutionary past, we had to 'fit in' with our community in order to survive the tricky landscape of predators, harsh weather conditions and food shortages from the land. This 'Tribal Affiliation' was literally what kept us alive, so it's no stretch to consider that over Millenia we have evolved to be much more cognitively intelligent and sophisticated, with agriculture and industrialization developing at a rapid rate, yet our poor minds and bodies unable to quite keep up with our levels of technological and societal advancement. We are still left with remnants of our prehistoric brain function that hasn't quite grasped the fact that we're no longer being chased by giant beasts or invaded by neighbouring tribes (at least not usually!)

That feeling of sheer terror and panic that we might be shunned or ridiculed, not accepted for who we really are, or, heaven forbid be totally inadequate and not measure up to the expectations of our fellow 'Tribesmen' – is exactly the same as if we were being chased by a beast, and our bodies mount the same response as if we were.

This, quite obviously gives rise to social anxiety, imposter syndrome, low self-worth, confidence issues, body dysmorphia, depression........you get the picture.

Our stress response is the most powerful tool we have as humans to jolt the body into action, and as you will see over the coming chapters, this is something that should be at the forefront of education, from early years to adult learning, plastered across the medical, education, fitness, beauty, fashion and media industries, due to the overwhelming evidence of prolonged exposure to stress hormones being one of the leading causes of mental and physical ill health, with countless studies of long term chronic illnesses being triggered and exacerbated by the hormones that we release during stress.

Of course that's not the case, as it serves a great purpose to keep people in a constant state of stress response – how else will the fashion, beauty, and pharmaceutical industries generate such profits?! (controversial I know! – doesn't stop it from being true!)

So, I think it's high time we start from the beginning and have a look at what's going on for you. Let's dig deep and uncover the real you. (hint: you might surprise yourself!)

We will start with a little self-portrait!

How do you see yourself?

Don't worry – you don't need to be a master artist, if you can manage a stick man you can do this. See what comes up when you start to scribble a representation of you. If you don't fancy drawing then write a list of all of the things that describe you.

Think about all of the words that describe you. What are the things that you dislike about yourself? What do you like? Is there anything that you like?

Who are you beneath all of your roles?

Write down here all of the roles you have to play on a daily basis (ie: parent, friend, sister, brother, boss, employee) – and then see what's left. What part of your life do you give to your own happiness and fulfilment? And how much is taken up with other peoples needs, wants and desires?!

What is your secret superpower? You know, the thing that you're really good at or would really love to do, but are afraid to tell anyone about?

How could you possibly share your gifts with the world? And what is the worst thing that could happen if you didn't hold back?

If you're finding it hard to think about anything other than what you're been conditioned to believe as truths about yourself then use the next page and fill in the blanks, see if that inspires you to think deeper about what makes you ....you!

Loves...

Hates...

Can...

Cannot...

Would like to..

Would never...

Is afraid of..

Gets angry when..

Feels happy when..

Gets excited when...

Is inspired by..

Secretly wishes they..

inhale confidence
exhale doubt

When we are little, we are often encouraged to do exercises like these. To dream without limits and pretend that we can be anything we want to be. Why do we suddenly stop doing this? Who tells us that we can no longer follow our dreams but need to 'get real' and start working towards a life of mediocrity, unhappiness and unfulfillment?

We will start to uncover subconscious programming further into this book, but for now, I'd just like you to ponder on the fact that throughout your life, your core beliefs about yourself have more than likely been programmed in by someone else – unwittingly, but nevertheless programmed in to your beautiful perfect brain, a list of disempowering, self-worth crushing, completely false statements that resonate with SOMEONE ELSE'S view of the world.

There is an extremely high chance that you have spent the majority of your time, since this childhood programming, believing these statements to be absolutely true, and worse still, finding subconscious ways to live up to these false beliefs and prove them right.

If you think back to your earliest memories, did a parent, sibling, friend or teacher ever tell you that you weren't very creative/sporty/clever/practical ...... the list goes on.

Or maybe you heard the words 'you're stupid, fat, ugly, skinny .... you get the picture.

Even harmless 'banter' where family and friends tease youngsters about having 'puppy fat' or being a bit 'dopey' have catastrophic, far reaching consequences that nobody could predict, until we managed to get a good grasp on neuroscience and human behaviour and start to unpick the damage.

Words are indeed weapons and we should choose them very wisely, as you will discover, your choice of language is crucial for uninstalling beliefs that damage you and programming in more positive ones, so please think on the next time you are about to utter a word or phrase to a loved one – especially a child. Even if it is just 'banter'.

Chapter 2: Stress & Our Stress Response

The word 'Stress' has it's origins in the Latin word 'Strictus', meaning 'drawn tight' – and that, to me is a great description of how we feel when under stress. Physical feelings manifesting in your body as huge red flags telling you that something isn't right. Drawing you in tight until all you can think about is the very thing that is causing those constricted feelings.

But why does it happen? Why do we feel those sensations? What purpose does feeling crappy serve?

In order to unpick the worst pandemic to hit modern civilization (no, not Covid-19, I'm talking about chronic stress) we need to go back to our evolutionary past.

As I have already mentioned, our chemical responses to stress date way back to when we were living in hunter-gatherer times, and we needed specific stimulus to warn us of impending danger from a predator. Our brains are truly amazing supercomputers which we still are nowhere near being able to understand, but thanks to modern science, and in particular Neuroscience, we have been able to gather a much greater understanding of how things work, and our brain's role in sending out a whole multitude of chemicals in response to various life situations, which cause us to feel, and react in certain ways.

I have been studying with fascination for the past few years, the fields of Neuroscience, Psychology and Human Behaviour and feel that I have scratched the surface just enough to be able to put into laymans terms, the magic that happens when we experience a PERCEIVED stress (note the word in capital letters – we will come back to that later).

Stress can be physical, chemical and emotional, and when we are knocked out of balance in any of these areas we turn on our 'stress response'. This is crucial in certain situations to keep us alive, BUT incredibly damaging when we can not turn the switch back off again.

When I explain this within a Mindset Mojo session, I always focus on three parts of the brain:

1. The Amygdala
2. The Hippocampus
3. The Prefrontal Cortex

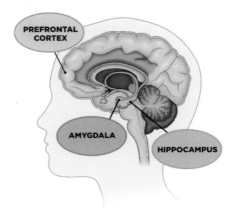

Now if you're anything like me, you will need something far more easy to understand than confusing Latin science jargon words or you'll immediately forget the important, sometimes life changing information that you are about to hear – and I want this stuff to become embedded in your minds so that the next time you experience a stressor, you can recall exactly what is happening inside you. So we are going to look at the 'animals in your brain' to make the explanation even simpler.

You will see my snazzy poster somewhere within the coming pages to remind you, but for now let's have a look at the three areas in more detail.

1. *The Amygdala*

The word *Amygdala* is Latin for 'Almond'- and so the name fits perfectly with the tiny gland in the middle of your brain that is shaped exactly like it's namesake. It's function is to act as your 'fear radar' and is hard at work day and night, even when you're asleep, picking up any signals through your senses that there may be a danger somewhere close. Think of it as your internal guard dog (or excited puppy might be a better analogy as it often sleeps with one eye open and jumps up barking furiously when it spots a piece of fluff on the floor)

Way back when, our amygdala was crucial for sending out the initial signal to the control centre of our brain to take action rapidly as something was very, VERY wrong. A series of neurotransmitters would race to give the information over and a knock on effect would then occur, with the final result (all within a split second) being hormones such as adrenaline and cortisol being released into the bloodstream in order to divert energy to where it was needed most, the arms and legs to be able to run away quickly or fight off the incoming danger. Cells would become inflamed and primed for repair even before we were caught to allow for the best possible chance of survival.

2. The Hippocampus

It's very inconvenient that the name of this part of the brain relates to a Hippo, as they are traditionally not known for their amazing memory power so it really messes up my diagrams – so we will link the Hippocampus to the Hippo's large grey cousin, the Elephant, who we all know does not forget anything at all. Ever.

The Hippocampus is basically the brains storage vault and is home to everything you have ever seen, heard, felt, tasted, experienced – it's all there stored away in a giant rolodex, just waiting to be recalled when it's needed the most.

We will be looking in more detail at the brain and its functions when we look at programming a bit further down the line, but for now, all you need to know is that you are only cognitively aware of a very small part of what's actually in there.

Your subconscious is incredibly powerful and actually makes up 95% of your mind. The remaining 5% is the stuff that it allows you to become aware of, if it thinks it's relevant to what you need at that time. Just imagine all of the things that are stashed away in there!

Have you ever experienced a smell or a song that takes you back and elicits a memory, or even a feeling that you can't quite put your finger on but you know there's something there in the back of your mind? That, my friends is the power of the subconscious mind. Your elephant is guarding a whole host of stuff that you are unaware of – not all of it positive, or helpful to you. The poor guy just knows it needs to keep hold of everything as a reference just in case it's ever needed again.

The trouble comes when we can't access logic and reasoning to work out whether what we're being presented with is actually relevant to us right now, helpful to the situation we're in, or indeed true. We need to be able to thank the big guy for doing his job so well, but find a way to get into the control system and find where all of the negative imprints from our past are being stored so that we can remove them and make some room for new, positive experiences that are in line with who we really are, and allow us to grow and thrive.

3. The Prefrontal Cortex

Now this part of the brain, with the snazziest name, is our most recently developed part, and is responsible for problem solving, language, logic, judgement and reasoning. It's what makes us 'human' in modern terms.

This guy is like the wise old owl of our brains and is always there, just like google, to tell us what to do in any given situation. The problems occur when we do not have an understanding of our perspective and perceptions. When we are looking through the lense of our past experiences, which often are projections of others people's 'stuff' onto us, we tend to have a skewed and distorted version of reality that's stuck somewhere in the past, from somebody else's perspective.

Because the emotional imprints or attachments from our past experiences, guarded carefully by our elephant, cause such strong physical, emotional and chemical reactions in our bodies, its often difficult for us to step back, view the situation from above, and recognize that these things often don't serve us any more, and are simply left over and stuck from experiences, interactions and relationships from the past.

When looking at the interaction between the animals, and our stress response, this is what happens:

When we experience a trigger that is logged somewhere in our subconscious, our guard dog has absolutely no idea what is a real danger and what is a perceived danger, he just knows by communicating with the elephant and finding something in the rolodex that made you feel bad before, that he needs to do something fast to stop it from happening again.

At this point, there seems to be a break in communication, and the guard dog sounds the alarm, the sprinklers go off, the sirens wail, the elephant hides in the cupboard and the owl flies away.

The only animal left to fix the problem is the one that we have absolutely no control over..........our Ape.

Now, if you have read the Chimp Paradox, by Professor Steve Peters, you will already have an understanding of how our minds work and some great strategies for getting control of this fella (keeping bananas and a cage handy is always a good idea) – if you haven't read it I highly recommend it and you can find more details in the recommended reading section.

Our Ape is the animal analogy for our 'Fight or Flight' response (or fight, flight or freeze response. There is actually a fourth 'flock' response but that's for later) – otherwise known as our sympathetic nervous system response.

As we've already discussed, in our evolutionary past, this guy was essential for survival, and if there was a grizzly bear on the horizon, or another tribe about to attack, it was essential for the guard dog to pick it up immediately, bypass all of the other parts which would slow us down by reasoning and questioning, and go straight to the big guns. Letting the ape out of the cage as quickly as possible was conducive to human survival in our past so these parts of the brain served a crucial purpose. We just need to learn how to use them wisely now that we have evolved so quickly and don't have the same dangers as we did before.

We used to spend hours by the fire in 'rest & digest' (or 'breed & feed') mode, which is the opposite to fight or flight. The switch was simply flicked on when it was needed and then turned back off again for the rest of the time which kept our bodies in 'Homeostasis' or balance.

Think of it as two sides of a coin. It is impossible to be in both states at any one time, you can only be in one.

Our highly civilized and modern society, where we think we have it completely right and are so superior and intelligent compared to our past, is actually completely and utterly OUT of balance, and it's getting worse. With the mental health crisis being at the forefront of every newspaper, programme, film, and social media post at the moment its glaringly obvious that we are not as great at life as we think we are.

We are stuck on a treadmill with that grizzly chasing us, constantly in fight or flight mode, with our sympathetic nervous systems working in overdrive 24/7 to protect us from an unseen danger. When we really look to the root cause of this, the majority of the fear we feel is from our perceptions. Fear of what we THINK people will think of us or say to us. What we BELIEVE will happen if we speak out or step away. We are trapped in constructs that relate only to our skewed past and other people's narratives (remember Dr Tim's advice at the beginning?)

In terms of cellular biology, more new science is revealing amazing new truths about what it means to be human, and how the structure of our cells is not actually what we originally thought it to be. With this new knowledge, comes the realization and resulting responsibility that we are in fact more than just bystanders in life, waiting for things to just happen to us, completely at the mercy of external sources and doomed to a path determined by our genetics.

We now know, for example, according to the wonderful Dr Bruce Lipton in his book 'The Biology of Belief', that the nucleus of our cells, which we used to think held all of the keys to 'US', is actually just a holding space for our DNA codes, our genetic blueprint that we are assigned at birth which holds all of the potential for everything we could ever be. Each cell holds the same coding, whether it's a hair cell, a liver cell, a skin cell or a brain cell – the difference comes from our wonderfully magical cell membranes which we used to think was pretty much cellophane wrap keeping all of our cytoplasm from spilling out.

We know now that it's the cell membrane that we need to pay attention to as it holds minute receptors that pick up the transmissions whizzing through your system, packed full of information to activate specific codes within the nucleus. This tells us that external factors such as our environment, play a major part in what information gets sent to these receptors.

Imagine for a moment that you are constantly exposed to toxic material through your place of work, where you live, your diet and of course the chemicals being released from your stressors when that guard dog goes crazy – this information is being continuously shuttled to every cell in your body where those magical cell receptors activate the DNA codes within the nucleus DEPENDING on what that information is. So if you are having an awesome day, eating good, nutritious food, getting sunlight, exercise and exposing yourself to the things you love and feelings of joy, love, and belonging, then your cells will be triggered to activate your highest possible vibration of optimum health.

On the other hand, most of us will be finding that we are constantly making choices that send information to our cells to react, inflame, and shut down. Sobering I know. But all is not lost as with this amazing new knowledge comes power, and we can use it to understand our own minds and bodies and make life changing choices, rather than the excuses our bodies can no longer afford to accept.

We live in a society where it's more common to use drugs (both prescription and illegal), alcohol, shopping, food, gambling, social media, and other distraction habits and addictions to plaster over the cracks, numb up from the reality of what's going on, and find temporary solutions to mask symptoms rather than get to the root cause and remove it completely, in order to live our best lives.

Now the pharmaceutical, alcohol, retail, fashion, media, beauty and food industries have a lot riding on the fact that we stay blissfully unaware of a lot of this information so it's no surprise to me that these things are not commonly shared within mainstream media, or found on curriculum materials for our schools, but that's a whole other story! I will leave that idea in your mind while we carry on with the good stuff, and you can use your new critical thinking skills to come to your own conclusions on that one.

For now, we will educate and empower ourselves as much as we can, work together with kindness, compassion and understanding, and find a way forward out of this quagmire of stress, anxiety, depression and despair and into a new space of positivity, resilience, strength and hope.

It's time to take the power back, grab that pen and start rewriting your future. Nobody else should have to power to decide what is good for you or what you should want, and we all need to get out of the perception that we are not enough, and need to people please and prove ourselves in order to be loved, valued and accepted.

With some simple awareness and brain training I truly believe its possible for us to break free of these chains, understand what's going on and where we have gone wrong, and empower ourselves and each other to undo some of the damage, and install some super self-care software in our super computers.

It's time to settle your ape down, work with your elephant, retrain your guard dog and have a good chat with your wise old owl.

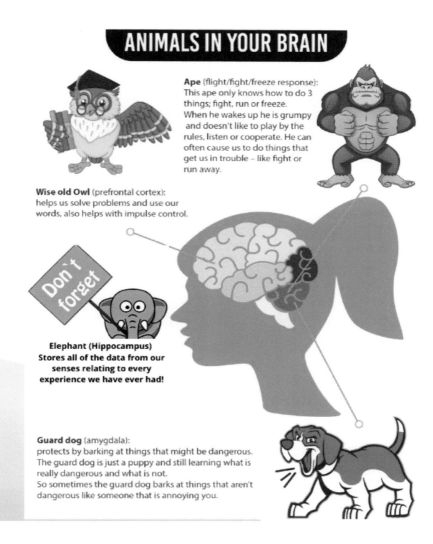

ANIMALS IN YOUR BRAIN

Ape (flight/fight/freeze response): This ape only knows how to do 3 things; fight, run or freeze. When he wakes up he is grumpy and doesn't like to play by the rules, listen or cooperate. He can often cause us to do things that get us in trouble – like fight or run away.

Wise old Owl (prefrontal cortex): helps us solve problems and use our words, also helps with impulse control.

Elephant (Hippocampus) Stores all of the data from our senses relating to every experience we have ever had!

Don't forget

Guard dog (amygdala): protects by barking at things that might be dangerous. The guard dog is just a puppy and still learning what is really dangerous and what is not. So sometimes the guard dog barks at things that aren't dangerous like someone that is annoying you.

MY AMAZING BRAIN

MINDSET MOJO

Prefrontal Cortex

Limbic System

Executive Centre:
'The Thinking Brain'

Handles:
- Focus
- Logic
- Judgment
- Organization
- Impulse control
- Learning from mistakes
- Problem Solving
- Self-Awareness
- Self-Regulation
- Attention
- Empathy & Compassion

Developmental shifts around ages 5-6, 11 & 15. Is said to mature around age 25.

Emotional Centre:
'The Emotional Brain'

Handles:
- Emotions
- Memory
- Response to stress
- Separation
- Anxiety
- Fear
- Rage
- Hormone Control & Social bonding

Developmental focus between 0-5 year with significant shift during adolescence.

Reptilian Brain

Survival Centre:
'Fight, Flight or Freeze'

Handles: Autonomic functions such as
- Breathing
- Digestion
- Hunger
- Sleep
- Heart rate
- Instinctual behaviours designed to sustain life

Developed at birth.

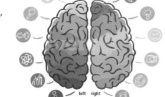

left brain   right brain

Now, there is some good news through all of the complicated Latin words and animal analogies. We have discovered that, contrary to what we originally thought, our brains aren't programmed in from birth without any room for change, but programmed in mainly through our experiences in the big wide world and our interactions with other people.

We now have so much exciting science coming out regarding something called 'Neuroplasticity' – which is the ability of the brain to literally rewire itself through identifying negative programmes, removing them, and programming in new thoughts and behaviours.

Think of it as a field full of corn with a path worn in. At first there seems to be no way through, but after a while of walking the same route you start to carve out a very clear path from A to B.

What we do through our lives is experience thoughts that trigger 'feelings' and our emotional responses then result in negative behaviour, and we continue this pattern time and time again until those particular neurons are totally hardwired together (neurons that fire together wire together!). You can see this in the case of children who learn to behave in a certain way, and build in short cuts that result in a trigger instantly causing a behaviour – their neurons are wired together through repetition, and this soon becomes a part of who they are, and a label then becomes attached to them like a stone around their neck for the rest of their lives (think about the 'naughty' kid in school)

What SHOULD happen is that the trigger, thought, emotion, feeling and resulting behaviour is identified, worked through and a new behaviour strategy put into place in order to break that connection and create new neural pathways for the more desired behaviour.

If you think about all of the negative thoughts and behaviours that are present in your life and just how much they hold you back, you can see over time how they have become embedded into your control system and you truly believe that they are just 'who you are', something intrinsically broken and wrong with you. All of those labels that you have been given over time, by other people and your own internal saboteur – really shouldn't be there, and they CAN be removed and replaced with something far more awesome and useful to you. THAT is neuroplasticity my friend.

Chapter 3: Comfort Zone or Prison?

So we have all heard of the expression 'comfort zone', in fact we use it constantly to excuse why we don't do things. If something is outside of your comfort zone, it sits outside of the self-imposed restrictions that we place upon ourselves based on our feelings and emotions connected to past experiences.

If we feel any unpleasant sensations in our bodies at all, this means that we are uncomfortable in some way – and that is unacceptable to us. We are constantly striving for perfection, joy, happiness and all of the warm fuzzies that come with pleasant things happening both inside and outside of us. This 'Perfection Trap' as I like to call it is based on the fact that there is in fact something universally attainable that we should all be working towards and anything else is bad and should be avoided at all costs.

The truth, as I have found on my journey so far, is that we need to follow the more Eastern based philosophy that we should embrace the dark as well as the light, and learn to acknowledge our emotions and feelings, both pleasant and unpleasant, recognizing that for every unpleasant feeling we experience, we will no doubt learn and grow, and that is the whole purpose of our very existence.

I can not think of a sadder life than one spent imprisoned in the constructed story that one needs to get up at the same time each morning, take the same route to work, to graft for 8 hours on the dot in order to line someone else's pockets, clocking out at 5pm, taking the same route home, to watch the same tv shows and drink the same bottle of wine or can of beer until its time to go to sleep and set the alarm to start all over again. Sleep, eat, work, repeat, until we are finally allowed to retire once we are too old and immobile to enjoy a life of any kind, ending up resigned to live out the remaining days reminiscing and regretting the poor choices we made and what could have been, until our final breath is taken and our hearts play their final beat.

What a tragedy

Yet that is what most human beings subscribe to, and pretend to enjoy the process, just because everyone else seems to be living their best lives on their social media highlights, and that's what society's narrative states we should be happy with.

Heaven forbid we rock the boat and upset the status quo by speaking out that we are actually feeling pretty crappy and unfulfilled, tired and exhausted with the daily grind and endless missed opportunities, wants, needs, dreams and wishes unfulfilled.

So why do we entertain the very idea of such a tragic existence, let alone subscribe to it?!

Fear.

Remember earlier on when I told you I would come back to the 'Flock' response in our sympathetic nervous system response? Well here it is. We are constantly living in fear that we are not good enough. We are unworthy of love & acceptance, our two most basic human needs that we seem to be on an endless, and fruitless search for.

We live in a near constant state of panic and anxiety that if people see the real us that we will somehow become unlovable, shunned, or laughed at, and so we buy into the endless institutional, societal and governmental constructed narratives that are paraded out as an assault to our senses on a daily basis, telling us who we should be, how we should behave and what we should like, which is then reinforced by our wonderful and totally non-toxic mainstream media, who of course have nothing but our best interests at heart. (Quick side note for those of you who miss my subtle attempt at humour through sarcasm)

It is through these filters that we create our view of the world and our place within it, and no matter what our heart tells us through our gut instincts about our truth, our pesky minds get in the way with the constant internal chatter, telling you that there's something inherently wrong with you if you don't act like everyone else, safety in numbers and all that. If we all flock together and behave in the same way like little lemmings, we will be safe from danger and all will be well.
Nothing could be further from the truth! If we continually deny our individuality, creativity, and truth as a sacrifice to the gods of media, consumerism and profit, then we are in real danger of suffering both mental and physical ill health, as I aim to show within the pages of this book.

If we live our lives confined to the prison walls of our comfort zone, never pushing our own boundaries of the unpleasant feelings of fear, then we will truly remain trapped in a life of monotony, disempowerment, sadness, longing and ill health, cunningly disguised as 'safety'.
Just to push your comfort zone a teeny weeny bit at a time, allowing yourself to feel some feelings that you have shied away from for so long, will allow you to learn and grow, and trust me when I tell you that once you have increased your comfort zone, it never goes back to where it was so you can continue to grow it and allow yourself more and more new experiences and adventures to lead you onto your true path. A path where you step out of fear and into your light. Once you reclaim and own your personal truth and remove the masks of fear you've allowed people to impose on you, you will never look back.

30

To delve a little deeper into the brain/body science behind the construction of our comfort zones lets think for a minute about our past experiences.

When we experience something in our lives that has a profound emotional impact on us we take a snapshot of it and store it away safely in our hippocampus where it becomes an important reference point for everything that comes after. When an experience is so strong that it elicits a serious emotional and physical response that you consider to be unpleasant, your mind makes a serious effort to protect you from ever experiencing that again, and that 95% subconscious comes into play again by reminding you with 'feelings' when it thinks that something is too close for comfort and may result in round two.

Most often this is completely irrational and based around a certain connection that your brain has made through its filter of experience as to what is important to you. Maybe a sound or a smell or a sight that is loosely related to the event, or even a picture of the person or event themselves – none of these things mean that danger is near and the experience is going to be revisited, but your trusty guard dog doesn't know that, and when he asks your elephant for a reference point to make a snap analysis, of course he throws up whatever had been experienced before and you go ahead and relive that all over again through the emotions, chemical reactions, feelings and behaviors that have been imprinted somewhere in your body for safekeeping.

This vicious cycle keeps you imprisoned in what you think is a zone of safety – preventing these things from ever happening to you again, when in actual fact what you are doing is living completely in the past and not allowing yourself any new experiences at all.

With some simple brain training, employing the neuroplasticity we mentioned before, we can really get into that growth mindset and create new positive experiences, the fulfillment of our highest dreams, wishes and desires and the manifestation of our greatest good. A life well lived with rich, fulfilling experiences and no regrets is waiting for you. You just have to take the action to go out and get it.

Exercise: The 'Vicious' and 'Vital' flowers exercise.

This is a good tool to use to see just how your negative thoughts have a massive impact on your feelings, emotions and resulting behaviour.

Take a piece of paper and draw two flowers (again, no spectacular artistry skills are needed – just the ability to draw a few shapes and stick them together)

The first one will be your 'Vicious' flower and in the centre I would like you to write a negative or limiting belief that you have about yourself.
This could be something like 'I am depressed'. Then I want you to use the petals to detail all of the resulting thoughts, feelings and behaviours that result from this one thought, such as 'I sleep a lot during the day and mainly watch TV' which results in being more tired and lethargic as well as insomnia at night, You might also put that you comfort eat a lot and this makes you feel terrible about yourself and reinforces your feelings of depression. You get the idea. Have a go and see how your vicious flower builds once you get going.

Once you have completed the first flower, it's time to reverse it and make your 'Vital' flower come from a more positive mindset and see what happens.

You could start in the middle with something like 'I am feeling more motivated' and then see what happens to the petals. You may find things like 'getting fresh air and going for a walk in the park' crop up, or 'focussing on healthier food choices', 'talking things through with a friend' and so on.

Even if you are not 'feeling it' at the time, this exercise starts the process of repatterning in your brain. When you write and read positive affirmations and suggestions they begin to programme in, and that is exactly what we want, so start using this exercise to write about how you would like to be feeling, and how that would change the landscape of your day for you. It will become your initial blueprint for future success.

Tackling Anxiety: The 'Doing it anyway' Model

This is another great exercise to start to reprogramme your brain to step out of the anxiety trap. We have already discovered the origins of the feelings that we experience and our rational brain can understand that more often than not, there is no real danger at all, just a PERCIEVED danger based on the filter of our past experiences.

Now that we have this knowledge it's important to take some simple, practical steps to start 'pruning' away at the synapses that link our triggers to our stress responses and the best way to do this is by gradually exposing ourselves to activities, experiences and events that would previously have stopped us in our tracks.

If we plan for this BEFORE things happen, our logical brain can take steps to prepare us for when the situation arises, and our subconscious can prepare us to take action that it may not have been prepared to allow us to do before.

Take some time to write down at least 3 things that you have missed out on doing, or prevented yourself from experiencing because they feel too scary.

Have a good look at what you've written down and analyse in detail, looking for real dangers and 'perceived' or 'imagined' dangers.

If you find that there is a real danger to your safety then obviously don't do it, but nine times out of ten when you think about the worst that could happen...... and the best – the pro's outweigh the cons. So what if you don't get it right? Who cares if people laugh? Really – is it worth missing something amazing?

Switching off Stress & Fear

Name the Fear

The 'doing it anyway' action

Name the Fear

The 'doing it anyway' action

Name the Fear

The 'doing it anyway' action

Chapter 4: Lobsters, Butterflies and Boundaries

During my search to educate myself on the subject of sneaky 'feelings' and why we feel some things as complete joy and happiness and others as total panic or misery, I have opened myself up to a brand new world of education, with subjects like Neuroscience, Psychology, Human Behaviour, Mindfulness and other spiritual based practices and philosophies, and even Quantum Theory of all things.

The fascinating insight into the human mind has left me speechless at times (impossible I hear you say!) – I am blown away at the complexity, power and downright magic that we humans hold, and even more blown away at the fact that this sort of stuff isn't common public knowledge (unless you're a Neuroscientist, Psychologist, Spiritual Guru, or Quantum Physicist of course!)

I have spent many hours writing endless scribbled notes, detailing the golden nuggets I have found during my research, trying to act as an interpreter of sorts, wading through the jargon and mind-blowingly complex language used in many texts. Simplifying things into the very basic lessons that I have learned and am now applying practically in my own life, with serious results.

Why wouldn't I want to share that with the world? I would love to see this stuff being made mandatory on curriculums across the globe, and can't fathom why it isn't already the foundations to our learning. My suspicion is that once we know too much about how much control we have over our own minds, then the narcissistic and tyrannical leaders we serve would no longer be able to keep our lights so dimmed. As Francis Bacon famously told us:

"Knowledge is Power"

One of my 'lightbulb' moments was when I was sat on my Air B&B bed, on my own at the back end of the Korean District of Manhatten, keeping my feet off the floor to avoid the mice (I kid you not). In an attempt to distract myself from the not so glamorous side of New York Fashion Week, I was on a quest to try and satisfy my thirst for knowledge and was researching the tricky subject of 'feelings' in an attempt to understand Anxiety, and why so many of the people I came into contact with these days were really suffering with debilitating anxiety, sometimes coupled with Depression.

The people pleaser that I am, I wanted to see if I could better understand, and maybe even find some coping strategies to share with clients, friends and family to help them to feel better.

I came across Rabbi Dr Abraham Twerski and watched a simple 2 minute video that literally changed the way I thought about 'unpleasant feelings' forever.

I have spoken about this ever since on many stages and within my coaching groups, and it is by far the piece of information that gets the most positive feedback and people remember, and even send me emoji's of!

Lobsters.

Yes that's right you heard me correctly!

The most important piece of wisdom that I can give you after years of research and self-development is a story about Lobsters. More specifically, how a Lobster grows.

So we all know that Lobsters have rock hard shells and pretty mean claws. Serious armour going on there, but have you ever thought about how they grow? I mean if the suit of armour that they need to protect them is so hard, rigid and impenetrable then how does the Lobster grow?

Well, you see the Lobster is actually really squishy and soft, and also happens to be a really clever, emotionally intelligent little creature. When it starts to feel uncomfortable and under pressure, it recognizes these 'feelings' as red flags that something isn't quite right and needs it's attention.

It pays close attention to those feelings of pressure, and of being uncomfortable in it's current situation, and uses them as red flags to highlight that it needs to do something in order to grow,

It breaks out of it's old, rigid, confining shell that's been holding it back, and it takes itself off and hides itself in the safety of a rockpool whilst it reflects, learns and grows a new and improved super-shell that allows it to feel more comfortable and free once again.

Every time it recognizes those red flags, it knows that even though it may feel unpleasant for now, it's really a blessing that allows it to learn and grow, and those feelings are temporary and will subside as soon as it pays attention to the cues and do what it needs to do.

In stark comparison, we humans (who are far superior and obviously way more intelligent than a simple Lobster) seem to have very little emotional intelligence at all, and spend so much time chasing perfection, faking it, and running away from anything that feels unpleasant that we completely miss our internal cues, which, ironically are the very things that will help us to achieve the real life joy, happiness and fulfillment that we are so desperately searching for.

If we could just get used to the notion that unpleasant feelings aren't actually 'bad', they are just part of our internal barometer that fluctuates between intense pleasant and unpleasant feelings, in order to keep us on our own true path and highest good for us.

When we feel the more pleasant sensations that we associate with happiness, joy, love, and excitement then we need to recognize that whatever it is that we are doing is most definitely part of our internal 'blueprint' for what's right for us.

When we experience the more unpleasant sensations associated with lower vibrational emotions such as fear, anger, hatred, and sadness, we are simply being shown that whatever or whoever is around us at that time is not serving us. We are being knocked off our path by unseen forces, and our super sensitive subtle energy system is picking that up and giving us a feeling as a big red flag that we need to make some changes to get back to where we are meant to be.

The great tragedy in my eyes, with this newfound Lobster knowledge, is that so many people living in 21st Century stress and drama spend their entire life handing over their power to others, in the hope that they can help 'fix' these feelings, when the feelings never truly go away until the root of the problem is removed.

Just looking at the statistics for the Mental Health decline of our species, the level of medication, at younger and younger ages, and the rising rates of suicide provide a stark and sobering picture that we need to wake up and pay attention to.

NOBODY knows what your highest truth is apart from you. Somewhere deep in your cells is the coded information that makes you the perfect version of you. The energetic blueprint that is just waiting to be unlocked through your interactions and experiences, guided by your subconscious awareness of what works for you and what doesn't.

When we spend a lifetime trying to prove our worth to others, to please them and try to fit in so that we can gain acceptance, to sacrifice our own happiness and fulfilment in the hope that someone else will gain theirs and approve of you, what we actually get is a lifetime of stress, anxiety, overwhelm, anger and sadness.

You deserve better than that. You deserve everything.

We need to reach the point in society where we can develop individual and collective emotional intelligence, understand that we need to embrace all of our experiences, feelings and emotions in order to learn, grow, and experience the gift of life. By learning to trust our intuition and be that Lobster, expressing gratitude for those big red flags guiding us and showing us the way, and feeling comfortable enough in our own skin that we can stand up and say 'Hey you know what, that's not actually working for me. I don't think we quite have the right fit here so I need to take some time out and reflect so that I can make sure I'm doing what's right for me'

If we can just stop freaking out at every uncomfortable feeling, and just sit with it. Feel it for a while and analyse what its trying to tell us. Avoid the temptation to ignore it or distract ourselves, and try not to hand over the power to someone else to try and fix the problem (don't forget that nobody else knows your exact blueprint but you – so others will be trying to fix you up from their perspective of what would work for them!)

One great way to start to do this is by looking out for feelings in our bodies, and behaviours that we exhibit that are sure fire signs that we are in fight or flight and our sympathetic nervous systems have been activated. If you can write down 3 physical sensations that you have when you experience anxiety, and 3 behaviour traits that you display, it makes it a lot easier to become that Lobster and look out for the red flags as soon as they come up.

For example did you know that there is a very simple and interesting fact to explain what happens when we feel 'butterflies' in our tummies? Dr Bruce Lipton has such a great way of simplifying some complicated chemical and biological responses and I just loved his explanation of this, which has helped me to recognize when I have flipped the switch into the danger zone and need to do something to bring me back into balance.

When we feel that strange feeling in the pit of our stomach, what is actually happening is that our digestive systems are actually shutting down, and it's the nerve endings restricting and closing down that we can actually feel! That's how powerful our sympathetic nervous system is. In a split second it makes the decision to close down every other system in the body that is using up precious energy in order to divert it to where it's needed.

After all, we don't need to be digesting food if we are about to be eaten by a bear.

At the same time, and perhaps the most concerning of all, our sympathetic nervous system makes the decision as to whether we actually need our immune system at the time of impending attack. The quick calculation results in the immune system being shut down temporarily as the energy needed to fight or run away is so great it takes precedence over all other systems. If you were in a tent nursing an internal infection with your immune system mounting a full attack, and suddenly a bear appears outside the tent, your body would choose fight or flight as a response over helping get rid of the infection, as the immediate threat is the most necessary to escape, with the view that once we have outrun or fought off the predator, we can get back to what we were doing before and rest up, letting the immune system kick back in.

So what happens when we are never out of fight or flight? Food for thought.

The hormone Cortisol, which is the chemical released alongside adrenaline, is so powerful, it is actually given to patients before they undergo an organ transplant, so that the immune system can be shut off and the chances of rejecting the organ reduced. It doesn't take much brain power to start to understand the implications of not taking the stress response seriously and actively taking steps to bring ourselves back into rest and digest. The fact that Cortisol has earned the nickname 'Death Juice' is all the proof you need to start making these important changes today.

Can you imagine if we had been taught this information and some practical skills from an early age? How different our lives would look? What if we could teach our children to look at things from this perspective? Could we save them a lifetime of negative programmes ruling their every move? Could we help them to avoid chronic illness and unnecessary pain? Many leading experts from the fields of Medicine, Science, and ancient Eastern practices all now agree this to be absolutely possible with the right mindset.

When it comes to the subject of our children, they have an even tougher time ahead than us. It's no secret that many of our children are already experiencing an increase in adrenaline addiction from gaming, with the fight or flight response in full swing from the digital stimuli. This has a knock-on effect that makes real life seem dull and boring in comparison and induces low level anxiety and over reactions to normal situations. Social interaction becomes blurred and translates into behavioural issues at home and school.

If we as adults haven't got the understanding of the mind/body/behaviour connection then how on earth can we help, guide and nurture our kids?

Simple strategies such as encouraging appreciation of the simple, free things, have a profound impact on our internal chemistry, and in turn our emotional regulation, behavioiurs and experiences.

As adults we have forgotten the simple pleasure of the sun on our face, the feeling of our bare feet on the grass, running as fast as you can for no reason at all, laughing out loud, and simply breathing and noticing your breath. If we no longer pay attention to these things, how can we expect our children to? Kids learn by example and we are not modelling particularly good behaviour. Believe me, our digital babysitters do not have our children's best interests at heart.

Setting healthy and appropriate boundaries is something that we should be instilling in our younger generations from as early as possible, but how can we even begin to think about this when we can not do it for ourselves?

I recently heard a fantastic piece of advice – when we actively practice self-care and self-love, we vaccinate our children against low self-esteem. This is so very true, and something that we all need to think carefully about.

Until we heal our own inner child and put together the broken pieces that exist deep within our subconscious, how can we help and guide our youth? We need to lead by example and walk the talk.

Once our young people start to see us challenging our own beliefs and perceptions, and working through our own 'stuff' in order to step into our value, speak our truth and honour ourselves, then the next generation, who are watching our every move for guidance and direction, will become empowered to gain their own sovereignty.

We have a duty and a responsibility to heal ourselves and spark our internal lights so that we can light the touch papers for the next generation.

We can't expect a child to foster healthy boundaries and choices if they are watching us do the exact opposite. It's time to wake up, shape up, stand up and not give up.

We can only start to create profound and lasting change when we follow the example of our friend the Lobster.

In his paradigm shifting book 'Power vs Force', Dr David R Hawkins takes us through over 20 years of in depth research (which we will look at in more detail later on) into our subtle energy attractor fields that resonate at certain levels depending on what we are feeling. His simple conclusion below helps us to start to understand how important it is to actually stand up and take notice of the feelings that we feel – after all, if we keep trying to distract ourselves, numb up, or pack them away in a box somewhere in our minds, they will simply wait for us, so why not take the power back and just let ourselves feel them? Process them and get them moving through and out so that we can learn, grow and get on with living our best lives?

"Stress is the net effect of a condition that you are resisting or wishing to escape" – David R Hawkins

Why do we spend so much time trapped in the self-imposed prison of stress, when evidence shows that we simply need to learn to recognize what it is that we are uncomfortable with and isn't resonating with our highest truth, and make the decision to move away from it?

My next challenge to you is to have a think about all of the recurring people and situations that you attract into your life that aren't serving you. What does this say about your past?

Can you write down some examples of unhealthy boundaries that you have in place at the moment? What can you do to shift these into healthy ones that serve you?

Combining new healthy boundaries with some internal spring cleaning is the way forward, and the next step on your journey to find your Mojo.

Chapter 5: The Mind-Body Connection

"I think, therefore I am"
- *Rene Descartes*

Unfortunately, about 200 years ago, modern medicine decided to chop the heads of the bodies of humans and treat each symptom as it arose, without considering the fact that brain chemistry had initiated that symptom in the first place (every single function of the body has to be processed and actioned through the super computer, from digestion and respiration to pain receptors and mutating cells). The brain is the command centre and once the decoding of the primary objective has taken place, snazzy little shuttles called neuro-peptides race through every corner of our body shooting back and forth sending messages to and from different parts with operating commands.

By simply treating a symptom chemically, mechanically or surgically as in our current medical model, there is no room for removing the cause, only for the treatment of symptoms as they appear.

The difference between 'treating' and 'healing' is that with treating, the context remains the same, so outward symptoms can be recovered from but often return and need a maintenance package.

Healing however looks to change the *context,* so absolute removal of the basis of the condition is the goal. There are many healing modalities throughout the world that have profound impacts on millions of people, and many well documented cases of 'spontaneous' recovery where in actual fact the big difference is the patient affecting the mind to remove the toxic patterns or 'beliefs' that resonate with disease so that the body follows suit and removes the symptoms.

"The invisible universe of thought and attitude becomes visible as a consequence of the bodies habitual response"
– Dr David R Hawkins

There are so many papers, books and resources on the subject, (my favourites will be detailed in the recommended reading and Bibliography section at the end), and Dr Hawkins findings eloquently sum up the power of our minds when it comes to our physical health.

By the time we get to the point of having a symptom picked up by the modern medical marvels of X-rays and scans, disease is well underway. Just consider the word itself 'Dis' 'Ease' – the state of not being at ease.

When we constantly respond to the stressors that we face in the same, unhealthy and uneducated ways, we find our bodies reacting with red flags more and more as they cry out for us to simply listen and act accordingly.

It was an amazing woman, Dr Candace Pert, a neuroscientist and pharmacologist who first discovered, or should I say re-discovered Mind-Body Medicine as a legitimate area of medical research. (ancient civilizations and their medicine men and women have worked with this model for generations until the new Western medical model deemed it 'quackery' and 'nonsense')

Dr Pert coined the phrase 'bodymind' and dedicated her life to research in this field. In explaining the magnitude of her findings she said ***"Since emotions run every system in the body, don't underestimate their power to treat and heal"*** – and I couldn't agree more

In fact I have spent the past 7 years on a mission that has taken me to Machu Pichu in Peru, and back to Wales with a renewed fascination in the self-inflicted limits that we put on ourselves, obsessively pouring over journals and volumes written by neuroscientists, microbiologists, quantum physicists and eastern mystics.

With my rudimentary and unsophisticated knowledge I have reached the following conclusion.

-Each specialist who narrows their field of study, spends a lifetime looking through a very specific lense, whether that is scientific, medical, philosophical, spiritual or religious. However in broadening my research into a multitude of areas at the same time, operating from a place of curious inquisitivity, instinct for truth, and as much mindfulness I can manage – I feel as though I have managed to pull the subtle gossamer threads woven silently between these areas, connecting them irrevocably, but just out of reach of those who descend into their own limited areas of study, research and academia. By failing to take a Holistic approach, the important realizations have been missed, until very recently, with the emergence of new and exciting discoveries and data from our modern sciences.

The second problem comes from the inability of the rational 'conscious' mind to be able to even begin to comprehend anything that is not able to be nicely boxed, labelled, examined and analyzed with our old, outdated Newtonian scientific model.

The irony here is that these brilliant minds exist so strongly in the 'Ego' space of our human selves that they never manage to transcend the veil and uncover the power and potential that is all around us, the way that the ancient Egyptians, Native Americans, Indian Sadhus and Budhist Monks did.

Believing that we are far superior and evolved with our brilliant minds, technological advances and scientific experiments we have lost the other part of us that complements our 'brains' so beautifully, our 'knowing' – that bigger part of us that is connected to something more. Call it our 'gut instinct' or 'sixth sense', there's nothing new age hippy mumbo jumbo about this stuff if we can get past the social constructs and narratives that have programmed in the belief that anything that can't be observed and classified with our five basic senses cannot possibly exist.

We can not see, hear, touch, taste or smell electricity to know and trust that it is there when we turn on a light bulb, or that gravity is in fact constantly present and stopping us from spinning out into the vast universe. So why do we find it so hard to imagine that there is another hidden element relating to our 'consciousness' that we have 24/7 access to, right in front of us, if we can just tune our radio dials in to the right frequency?

I have mentioned Dr Bruce Lipton before, and his amazing book 'The Biology of Belief' has had a profound impact on me, to the point that I really can't stop researching similar findings, as the implications give me so much hope for the future.

He talks of we humans as being mere skin covered petri dishes, with colonies and communities of different organisms carefully calibrating and working harmoniously together in perfect balance.

When we do a little research its easy to see that accuracy of this statement. We view ourselves as a whole, human being, who is merely participating in life with zero control over what happens to us. Simply at the whim of genetics and fate, on the rollercoaster of life, trying to hang on and make it to the end of the ride in one piece. (this turns out to be a really strong and convincing excuse as to why we relinquish our power and accept the belief that we have no control over what happens to us as it's much easier to lay the blame for our misfortunes squarely at somebody or something else's feet than to accept the realization that we are in fact fully accountable!)

Realizing that each and every cell is sentient, intelligent, and contains the exact code or blueprint to our full potential is an awe inspiring discovery, which opens up the potential for a completely different life to emerge from the one you are currently living.

I can tell you first hand that by discovering this kind of knowledge myself, I immediately started to discover ways to try and test the theories, implement new strategies into my life, and continue to see results that I never had believed possible, all the while furiously scribbling down my findings and experiences along the way, to satisfy the compulsion that I would need to put it all into a book someday to share this life changing stuff with as many people as I could encourage to listen.

Dr Bruce's realization in a moment of clarity during his career, that we are in fact, akin to television sets, and that actually what we play out with our bodies on a daily basis, has to in fact come from a frequency *somewhere else* that is simply being received by our brains, chemically decoded and transported to the rest of our cells, tells us exactly the same thing that I have read in countless books and papers from scientists to spiritual masters.

We are more than just our physical selves.

Science has held on to the belief kicking and screaming for so long that we are just machines that have learned how to think, when in actual fact, the new science that is emerging mirrors the ancient wisdom that we are in fact *thoughts that have learned to create a physical machine.*

Now I know that is going to be a very difficult statement to get your head around right now, especially as I've has years of studying to back this claim up, and now that I've just thrown it out there at you unexpectedly you may either think I've gone stark raving mad OR your mind has been similarly as blown as mine was and is now searching for a rational explanation.

Either way I encourage you to read on, as I have so much to share with you, and think of it this way – it will either be light entertainment for you or it will change your life. Winner Winner either way I'd say.

One of the books I really enjoyed reading and digesting was 'Quantum Healing' by the legendary Deepak Chopra, M.D.

I always love reading the words of doctors who, despite their years of intense medical training to the contrary, somehow manage to see past all of the traditional dogma of the old school medical model they once trusted implicitly, and realized that it's simply a collection of experiences that people have had and used them to form explanations and patterns, eventually forming indoctrination, which then becomes law.

Such medical professionals who feel that there is something more than simply questioning the patient, not to find out what is wrong with them, but to collect a series of symptoms that they can match to a classified disease in order to prescribe the number one chemical or surgical treatment to stifle the symptoms, fill me with hope for the future. The idea that person-centred, holistic medicine will eventually move us past the old, often barbaric, aggressive treatments which merely plaster over the cracks, and to a place where we can truly focus on what is causing the symptoms to show up in the first place is bringing us to a point in time where we can make a collective leap in consciousness and shift our mindsets completely. (*I am not suggesting that there is no place for modern medicine, merely that we need more of a balance in modalities, with pharmaceutical and surgical interventions focused on the trauma, field medicine and genetic conditions that it is so brilliantly designed for, and the chronic diseases manifesting through symptoms which may present in previously healthy people throughout life, be looked at with a more holistic, person centred lense, with emotional trauma as the first port of call for healing the root cause. You will understand my reasoning for this as we move further into the psychology/biology debate)

We always need to remember that symptoms are clues, or red flags, that let us know that there is an imbalance somewhere in our ecosystem and that needs our attention. Whether that's a sensation of anxiety felt in the gut, heart pains, or a cancer – there is always a reason for these things to appear. They do not spring into being by magic – our brains have received a signal from somewhere which distorts the decoding of our cells and tells them to do something abnormal.

The Mind-Body connection is a beautiful symphony with your pituitary master gland acting as the conductor, mobilizing a huge amount of complex chemical reactions instantaneously in order to keep us alive and in balance.

If you remember back to our fight, flight or freeze, animals in the brain analogy, I'd like to delve a little bit deeper into the truly amazing power that we have at our disposal. One that neither science or medicine can manage to put into a model, which frustrates them no end, as this is how they work. Of course models are useful, but as Deepak Chopra states, they have holes in them and only work when things are frozen in time, static and observable, not with dynamic change and evolution which of course are constantly moving and changing.

Take for example, when you are startled by a loud noise.

The 'thought' of fear creates a neuro-chemical. This trigger is the burst of adrenaline from your adrenal glands which sit upon your kidneys. This chemical then runs through your bloodstream sending messages all over the place, to your heart which then pumps harder and faster and elevates blood pressure, to your liver which puts out extra fuel in the form of glucose, to your pancreas which secretes more insulin to metabolise more glucose, and to your stomach and intestines which immediately stop what they are doing and shut down in order to mobilise more energy to where it's needed to escape the immediate threat (remember those butterflies?)

    All of this happens in an instant, as soon as one of your basic senses, in this case your ears, comes across a stimulus (the loud noise). It is the subsequent *thought* that starts of the chain reaction.

If you're still not convinced, there is a cool trick that I learned at a conference in London a few years ago. It was something that psychologists were using as a 'convincer' when explaining the mind-body connection to other medical professionals who were still caught up in the old school medical model.

Indulge me for a moment if you will.

Clear your mind for a moment (when I do this in one of my seminars I get people to close their eyes for maximum effect, but clearly if you do that you wont be able to read the instructions so just roll with it)

I want you to use your imagination and bring to the front of your mind the image of a lemon.

A nice, ripe, juicy lemon. Bright sunny yellow, with its shiny, dimpled, waxy skin and its citrusy aroma.

Now imagine for a moment that you have in front of you a chopping board and a very sharp knife.

I want you to score down the middle of the lemon and watch as a fine burst of juice sprays from the surface and the aroma strengthens. You take a deep breath and your nostrils are filled with that deliciously fruity, sharp tang and you just cant wait to cut it in half.

Listen as the knife chops through the juicy flesh and watch as the two halves separate onto the chopping board.

You notice droplets of juice running from the glistening segments inside and rolling onto the chopping board in all of their sticky glory.

You place a finger in the puddle of fresh lemon juice that has now formed on the board and bring it to your mouth.

As your finger gets closer the aroma is sharp in your nose.

You connect your finger with the tip of your tongue and the sensation explodes in your mouth.
Now

Observe what just happened in your body.

You will no doubt have experienced a physical sensation. Most likely a sharp sensation in your jaw as your saliva glands released a flood of saliva in anticipation of the lemon.

There is no lemon.

What happened was that a thought planted in your mind, recognised an experience that you have had previously with a lemon, and recalled with absolute precision all of the qualities associated with it. Right down to the complicated series of chemical reactions making you salivate.

All from thought alone.

-Incidentally, the molecules in your brain right now are not the same ones that will have previously experienced what we know as 'lemon' as your cells renew constantly, so these are brand new molecules that have never experienced 'lemon' before – yet the exact coding exists somewhere in the ether, a complete blueprint for the experience that is 'lemon', just waiting for you to draw on it again. Mind blowing? Absolutely, but we will come to that later.

Now it was commonly thought of before the 1970's that the reactions in our brain were purely electrical, until the discovery that there were also chemical responses that caused the resulting activity in the body. This brand new discovery, that neuro-peptides (or floating intelligence that can travel anywhere in the body), actually existed and acted as little mini messengers shuttling chemical instructions and 'talking' to all of the other cells in the body using the language of emotion, was a monumental discovery for the mind-body connection, particularly as 200 years before, science and medicine had effectively removed the brain from the body.

For years we have been operating under the assumption that anything to do with 'matter' was the dominion of medicine and science as it could be observed, weighed, measured, experimented on, and classified.

Anything to do with 'mind' was way too abstract and tricky to control so with no real explanation or ways to measure and experiment, this was given over to the realm of the unknown, and classified with spirituality and religion, and so the important connection was lost.

There is no better evidence for the power of the Mind-Body connection than that of the numerous cases of spontaneous remission from terminal diseases such as cancer, and the placebo/nocebo effect.

You don't have to take my word for it – you can look up the many cases of patients 'miraculously' recovering from Cancer at the 11th hour with all traces vanishing and no medical explanation.
They all have the same thing in common – a profound shift in their awareness, or consciousness. All patients had a moment of profound realization that they had the power and control to determine the outcome and no longer wanted to live in pain and fear. In new science speak, they achieved a quantum jump in their consciousness which allowed them to start operating from a place where the cancer could not exist. The subsequent codes sent via the brain's chemical responses was to shift the distorted coding in the malignant cells back into balance, which then resulted in the 'miraculous' and 'spontaneous' disappearance of symptoms.

Now, clearly this all happens on a very deep subconscious, in fact unconscious level, so to feel that we should somehow blame ourselves or that we have 'chosen' to be sick is the wrong way to think of it. Rather that we have not been given the full story or the information we need to empower ourselves to create the changes we need to get back into balance.

We are now starting to cognitively scratch the surface of the instinctive 'knowing' that our ancient ancestors had, that we have at our disposal all of the information and resources that we need for optimum health and life experiences. The irony is that we are now so preoccupied with social constructs, skewed beliefs, and the stories we constantly tell ourselves from our past emotional traumas, that we can no longer connect the two sides of ourselves together. Our conscious mind always seems to win out, even though it is the smaller part of our mind by a whopping 95%, our ego's keep control of the wheel.

One of the best patient experience recollections in 'Quantum Healing' is that of a lady who had presented with abdominal pain and jaundice symptoms. She had been referred in for surgery with suspected gallstones, but when they opened her up, they saw that she had a large tumour along with pockets of cancer dotted throughout her insides. Rather than operating, the surgeons simply closed her back up.

Her daughter, obviously distraught, begged them not to tell her, and so they told her they had in fact found gallstones and removed them, discharging her to the care of her daughter.

Expecting that she would not last the month, they were amazed when she showed up the year after for a routine check-up. Her explanation was that, when she had first gone in to the doctors office she had been so convinced that she had cancer, that when she found out it was only gallstones and that they had been removed, she swore to herself that she would never be sick another day, and relish life.

Upon examination, there was no sign of either gallstones, or any of the cancer. The power of the mind over the body is truly spectacular.

The same can be said in reverse, with the 'nocebo' response, something that I have witnessed personally with a loved one. Upon hearing that there is no hope and the prognosis is dire, many patients take that belief and programme it in as truth, and those neuro-peptides get to work transporting the chemical programming required for the mutation and destruction of cells.

This is even apparent in surgical procedures, with unconscious patients overhearing that the findings were worse than originally thought, statistics show the negative outcomes even when suggestion is made at a subconscious level, with positive talk during surgery showing to have the opposite outcomes in terms of patient recovery. So much so that it is now standard practice to not make any negative comments during surgical procedures.

There was even a case of a man at a hospice who was not expected to survive the day. The priest was called to administer the last rites and the patient died as soon as he had left the room. The trouble was that the priest had got the wrong room! The man he had seen was not expected to die at all, but the power of belief from this one act was enough to programme in a set of instructions to override everything else. Interestingly, the other man waited another three days for the priest to get to him!

So now that we know about our hidden abilities to transform thought into chemical reaction, creating and affecting physical matter, what does this mean for our future?

In terms of medicine, the exciting discovery that the living body is the best pharmacy ever devised is something that we really need to get out there into the mainstream. Knowledge is most certainly power, nevermore so than in this case.

We have the uncanny ability to create diuretics, painkillers, tranquilisers, sleeping pills, and antibiotics in exactly the right doses, administered at exactly the right time, all with the complete instructions built into its own intelligence.

No drugs company in the world can ever replicate this beautifully coordinated, elegant and sophisticated response, with very few (if any) side effects, in fact, when we try to replicate this in a lab, what we get is an uncoordinated, chaotic and often irreversible job, with no intelligence at all – just an assault on our finely calibrated ecosystem.

This is why we experience powerful and lasting side effects when we are injected with a man-made substance which, although does the job quickly, isn't cooperating or 'talking' to the other cells, just flooding our entire system in the hope that it hits the mark.

When our own natural healing systems are activated, the mind sends the chemical messages via the neuro-peptides, which always find the exact cells and give the exact doses of the exact substance (sometimes several different ones in several different places simultaneously), with the complex and sophisticated 'lock and key' system found on the cell membrane. These sticky receptors have exact fittings that work in the exact combinations to give the desired effect, and what's more, our brain-body connection also knows when and how to switch it back off again – something that no drugs will ever be able to do.

Of course this information is incredibly unhelpful to the pharmaceutical companies who have held the monopoly over our health (or lack of), and have the unwavering trust and hope of the general public, a high proportion of the medical profession, and the governments that they financially support.

The good news is that more and more people, like myself, are starting to use their instincts and their discernment to dig a little deeper and find out what they can do to empower themselves to take control of their own lives, rather than continuing to hand their power over to others.

The even better news, is that so many doctors and scientists, like the amazing, pioneering humans mentioned in this book, are speaking out and sharing the knowledge that blends both east and west, mind and body, together, and with logical and rational explanations that satisfy the scientific mind, whilst sitting in synergy with ancient healing and spiritual practices that have long been considered 'mumbo jumbo' and 'quackery'.

I need to reiterate here that I am in no way suggesting that there is no place for chemical and surgical intervention – these inventions have saved countless lives and will continue to do so, but are also freely handed out to anyone and everyone who exhibits a symptom, without taking into account any other modalities, including the now widely evidenced power of the human mind.

My point is that we now know that we have other options, and that drugs and surgery should be considered only after all other avenues have been explored – not as a first line of defense, and certainly not used as a commercial model with excellent marketing campaigns to keep people sick, depressed, and oblivious to the power inside them, for the purposes of lining pockets and obtaining power and status.

We have to learn to look at the whole picture and treat the body through the mind as well as the mind through the body.

I will leave you with one more thought to ponder on as we come to the end of this chapter.

"I think, therefore I am" takes on new meaning when we view it through the lens that Bruce Lipton was using when he realized that he was just the 'receiver' and that the real spirit of 'himself' was a frequency being transmitted from somewhere much bigger. For me, this thought leads me to the same comforting realization about death, as he mentions in his book.

If our essence, or 'soul' is a unique and specific frequency that comes in as thoughts, that in turn create matter so that we can have a series of experiences that we call 'life', then not only is physical death no longer as scary, but it opens up a whole new series of possibilities that were previously unavailable to us. We just need to learn more about it and experiment with methods of reaching out and connecting in with our higher selves so that we can actively create our experiences, rather then just passively accept what happens to us.

We are just starting to realise the startling and exciting/scary fact that both our mind and our body, as we have discovered so far, are both machines, we now need to learn more about the driver, to tap into the unique frequency of our higher consciousness so that we can access this beautiful quantum field of possibilities that has always been right at our fingertips!

Chapter 6: Heart-Brain Coherence

Nobody explains Heart-Brain Coherence better than Dr Joe Dispenza. One of the areas that I am so passionate about exploring and developing, I really believe this to be the key that will unlock our true potential, and the foundation for the concept of Mindset Mojo (even before I had heard of the term).

Dr Joe Dispenza was a Chiropractor running a practice in California, when at the age of 23, whilst engaging in a Triathlon, he was run over by an SUV.

He broke 6 vertibrae, and now considered this to be his greatest blessing.

After being told that surgery was his only alternative to paralysis, Joe embarked on an incredible journey of self-discovery and self-healing and now inspires millions of others to step out of their limiting beliefs and do the same.

In his book 'Breaking the Habit of Being Yourself' he goes in to great detail about the Heart-Math institute, and the thousands of experiments that participants have undergone in order to test the theory of the power of bringing the heart and the brain into perfect alignment and get them working together.

Have you ever found yourself saying 'I hate myself!'?

Have you ever wondered who those two people are? Who is this 'I' who hates 'Myself'?

These two entities can be described as your conscious and subconscious mind. Two parts to your whole self that need to learn to cooperate and collaborate in order to reach perfect balance and harmony.

James T. Mangan in his book 'The Secret of Perfect Living' (which we discuss within my Vibration Elevation Programme), likens the conscious mind, the smallest part which operates only 5% as the over confident office junior, who comes in operating solely from ego, with very little experience, but likes to think he's in charge and calling all the shots.

The Subconscious mind, making up 95% is likened to the CEO of the company, with a wealth of knowledge and experience, who sits back and lets the office junior flex his ego muscles until it's time to rein him in.

In this case, think of your conscious mind office junior as your brain centre, and your subconscious CEO as your heart centre.

Most of the time they are operating on different levels, at different rates, through different filters and with different experiences.

The trick is to get them operating in complete harmony so that the logic and reasoning of your conscious mind is communicating and cooperating with the intuition, wisdom and connected intelligence of your subconscious heart.

I left you with a thought before, about who is actually in the driving seat of your brain-body machines? Well your office junior likes to think that it is, but in actual fact your subconscious CEO is the part that is connected to the bigger 'quantum soup' of universal consciousness or intelligence, and acts as the bridge between the expansive sea of possibility found within the quantum field (more about that later!), and the cognitive processes that our office junior actively 'thinks' about, which as we now know, 'projects' these thoughts on to the body and creates our reality through a series of chemical responses.

Modern humans have the terrible affliction of believing that they are in full control, and that bad things are just 'happening to them', when in actual fact they are simply cut off from their subconscious through the brain patterning that has become wired in through past experience, and stored as an emotional imprint that repeats itself over and over again through the power of belief, thought and chemical reactions.

If only we could recognize that by connecting back in with our subconscious, we could actively select those thoughts, and allow the CEO to take the wheel, using its wisdom, experience and connection to the source of consciousness to rewire and reprogramme us back to optimum health and peak experiences.

Joe Dispenza, along with the Heart-Math Institute, conducted a series of experiments (and continue to do so), where participants were wired up to ECG machines which would measure their brain waves and their heart output.

Normally these two frequencies are completely mismatched and working against one another. No compatibility, and the resulting feelings and behaviour of this in our bodies is the feeling of stress, imbalance, fear, overwhelm – all of the unpleasant stuff.

By engaging in meditative practice, deep breathing, mindfulness, stillness and focusing on bringing the two into alignment, the data from the ECG's show the patterns starting to fall into synch with one another and bringing the person into greater awareness and a higher state of consciousness.

This links beautifully with the Law of Attraction which states that as soon as you have clear intent (coherent brain) with elevated emotion (coherent heart) you can literally attract anything you desire into your life.

This has gone from being an abstract notion to a clinically observed, measured and evidenced fact, opening up the possibilities for every human being to transcend the limits previously constructed in their own minds.

Viewing the brain (or thought) as the electrical charge and the heart (feeling) acting as the magnetic charge, you are literally sending out your wishes or intention for yourself out into the universal field of infinite possibilities, and drawing that reality back to you, utilizing the chemical reactions and mechanical processes that create matter and allow you to physically 'be' and 'do'.

It was in this way that Joe completely healed himself of his broken back without surgery. By focusing all of his intention and elevated emotion on the exact blueprint of his perfect spine, and committing to this with all of his being, his cells began to decode the DNA blueprint for the perfect spine that had always been there, and the bones, nerves and tissues all began to move his biology from living in the past to respond and heal and create a new future.

He then began the search for others who had managed the same kind of 'miracles' and soon found that in all cases, there had been a clear and focused intent, matched with an elevated emotion, and these were always elevated emotions of love, compassion, gratitude, unity and joy (kinda hard to do when you are at the bottom of the pit eh!)

The point is, it works, and if it works for thousands of others, then it can work for you.

Whilst conducting the experiments, what really stood out to me was the fact that the people operating the ECG machinery could soon predict when the subject was going to hit the critical mass point of elevated consciousness by tracking the activity in their brain. There was literally a point when coherence was achieved and the brain literally 'lit up', showing without a doubt that we are capable of elevating our consciousness to levels we have previously not experienced, with profound results.

I have seen footage of several of their mass meditations where hundreds of participants at a time are rigged up to the machinery and the resulting data combined with their testimonials and obvious blend of peace and elation speak for themselves.

I have obviously been experimenting myself with this, and have found some amazing results personally, blending a unique recipe of the techniques mentioned in this book, in various combinations depending on what I feel is needed at the time. A bit like a self-directed prescription just for me.

Having been an energy healer for over 20 years, it wasn't such a stretch for me to understand the power of the 'invisible' and to work towards refining my skills in connecting or 'tuning in' to the particular station that 'turns on' the energy flow for me.

The difference is, having a comprehensive toolkit rather than just one modality, I am now able to discern what is needed and when, and am learning to use these new skills to actively create my reality rather than just being a participant in a stressful game of chance that I have no control over – and I can tell you, it feels great.

Even when I hit roadblocks and challenges, I can now get excited that I am on the path for growth, and that every experience contains some knowledge that I need and a lesson waiting to be learned. It's such a comfort to know that all of the things that I feel I've 'known' instinctively, and followed with unwavering faith, in the absence of hard evidence, and even when others ridicule and scoff, is now becoming provable with some real explanations and hard evidence.

As Joe commented in a recent post praising the HeartMath Institute, ***"By using science as the contemporary language of mysticism they have elegantly married age old wisdom with their latest cutting edge research, and provide us with the tools to begin our own journey into heart intelligence"***

That inner part of me, connected to an ancient wisdom, that intuitive knowing that I could in fact connect in to something 'more' and harness and direct it to heal people, is now something that I can speak openly about, and build into a comprehensive programme, combining my own experience and research with the tools and strategies that have worked so well for me.

To end this chapter I'm going to leave you with a heart-brain coherence meditation so that you can experience it for yourself.

The best way to engage in this particular activity is to use your smartphone to record yourself reading the words, slowly, calmly and surely and play them back to yourself whilst sitting in a comfortable position with your eyes closed so that you can concentrate properly. (alternatively you can find my recorded version on my YouTube channel so you can just plug in your headphones and you're good to go!)

Heart-Brain Coherence Meditation

Sitting in a comfortable position with your back supported and your feet flat on the ground, close your eyes and take a few deep breaths.

Notice your breath as the air rushes in, and feel where it hits the back of your nose and throat.

Follow it's journey down deep into your lungs and notice as they expand with every breath in, and contract and empty with every breath out.

As you sit comfortably, bring your awareness to the top of your head. Can you feel your hair? Can you focus your awareness to the space that your head occupies, the space around it, and the space of the room that you are in?

Now focus on the very tip of your nose. Your eyelashes. Your hairline, where the skin of your forehead meets that first line of hair.

Focus your awareness back up to the top of your head, and follow it up to about 6 inches above your crown.

I would like you to visualize a beautiful glowing white ball of light, just hovering in that space. Your own personal sun. There for you whenever you need it, to energise you and fill you up.

Imagine as you take your next breath in, that you are breathing in this light through the top of your head, and as you do, it flows in and starts to fill you up.

From the soles of your feet, right the way up your entire body, you are being filled up with beautiful, healing, light energy.

Every cell in your body and all of the spaces in between are saturated with this beautiful glow.

As you bask in the feeling of pure light energy and the warm, peaceful glow that it brings, I would like you to place your hands on your heart space, one on top of the other.

As you take your next breath in, direct your awareness, and the light energy to your hands, and imagine that you are breathing in through your heart centre.

As you breathe out, you breathe through your heart centre. Repeat this process for a few minutes and sink into the wonderful feeling of love and compassion that this brings.
Send a wave of gratitude to your heart centre, and your heart itself for continuing to beat and keep you alive and vital even when you aren't aware. Send some healing vibes of love towards your heart centre and know that you are love, and you are loved.

When you are ready, ask yourself the following question:

What do I need to let go of right now in order to move forward with my life?

Do not judge what comes up. Your connected heart knows your truth, you just need to be open to listen.

Now ask the question:

What do I need more of in my life right now to bring me joy and fulfillment?

Ponder on this for a moment and recall the last time you felt the sensation of joy, fulfillment, peace, happiness and love.

Let this memory fill you up as you recall the sounds, sights, smells and sensations.

Remind yourself that you have permission to feel this way any time you choose, and can recall this feeling at will.

Set the intention that from this moment on you are going to release what is no longer serving you, and actively bring more of what gives you joy and fulfillment into your life.

Thank your heart centre once again, and release your hands.

Breathe comfortably for as long as you would like to remain in this elevated state, and when you are ready, wiggle your fingers, lightly stamp both feet on the floor and roll your shoulders.

When you feel that you are back to your previous level of consciousness, continue with another few deep breaths while you ground yourself back into the present.
You can do this either by imagining roots, like those of a tree, sprouting out of your feet and burrowing into the earth. Connecting you with the present and grounding you back into this reality. Or you can imagine securing a red anchor to each foot and sending them down into the centre of the earth, where they embed in the earth's core and keep you securely grounded.

Open your eyes and take your time getting up.

Remember to drink plenty of water and journal your experience, paying particular attention to any thoughts, feelings and emotions that came up, as well as setting out your clear intent.

Chapter 7: Losing Control

The single most difficult thing that we can do in life, is relinquish control and simply let go.

It also happens to be the single most important thing that we can do for ourselves to free ourselves from all of the traps that we find ourselves stuck in, the ones that create no end of damage to our mental and physical health, as well as our relationships.

We need to understand the concept of control. Of the things that we can and can't control, as well as the things that we should and shouldn't try to control.

A good example is the notion that we can control other people's actions if we can just try hard enough to please them more. Or the idea that we can control external situations as they unfold.

The only thing that we can truly control is our own reactions. Our own thoughts, feelings and behaviours – and we can choose to make these positive or negative ones in any given situation.

If we weren't so obsessed with what other people are doing or thinking then we might actually be able to see that we are always either making choices or excuses, literally all of the time. We choose our every thought, all be it unconsciously 95% of the time. When we find ourselves in a situation that we don't like, we then deny that we have made any such choice and instead we make an excuse. Anything will do, as long as it gets rid of that pile of accountability sat squarely at our feet. "Here, you have it – you made me do it", it's laughable when you break it down and think about it, and tragic in equal measures.

What if we could take full responsibility for all of our choices and actions and fight past our ego into the realm of the bigger picture?

We are so preoccupied with the ego self – that office junior always needing to be right, even with no experience and very limited knowledge. That creeping fear that someone will suss us out and realise that we really aren't cut out for the job and that someone else will be far better. The panic that people are going to judge and ridicule us at any moment if we admit one single bad decision or mistake.

Better to keep up the pretence that we know everything and blame someone or something else than take that chance. It's just too uncomfortable to consider that all of the things that are happening are a direct result of our own thoughts, choices and resulting actions. Our constant fight or flight response sees to it that we stay locked in the control trap.

What would happen, I wonder, if we decided to stop trying to control everything and just let things be?

What's the worst that could happen?

And the best?

Sometimes when we hold on to something too tightly we fail to see that it's actually damaging us, so the trick here is to take 5 steps back and put yourself in a place where you can view things from a birds-eye perspective, for a bigger view, a little perspective, and as little judgement as we possibly can,
Just contemplate all of the things that you can and do control, and then look at the things that you have no control over and really need to let go of. It truly is liberating and some serious weight lifted I can tell you.

So your task for this chapter is to make a list, with three columns

1) The things I can control
2) The things I can't control
3) The things I can now let go of

Once you've done that we can move on to the next sticking point.

Other people.

Have you ever thought about the people and things that have control over you?
Is there someone in your life that maintains a vice like grip over what you can and can't do? Maybe there is somebody around you who uses emotional blackmail to control your behaviour to match their needs, and you've never realized it before.

Or perhaps you struggle with social anxiety or phobias to the point that you avoid places or situations.

Let's critically assess all of the things that tie us up and stop us from connecting with our higher selves. What or who is it that keeps us locked into a place of stress and fear. Cut off from the higher vibes that allow us to feel joy, love, gratitude and create our perfect reality.

Where do we find the most toxicity in our lives, and most importantly, what steps can we take today to either get rid of them completely, or put better boundaries in place so that they no longer control us.

I have no doubt that the remaining chapters in this book will challenge the tight control that you have over your mind. Those programmed in beliefs from childhood, school, and years of social conditioning.

The heavily controlled idea that we already know absolutely everything there is to know with our superior science and technology, and that Newton and Darwin were both 100% accurate with no room for further development.

My challenge to you, is to explore 'letting go'.

See how it feels just to let go of pre-conceived ideas, thoughts and beliefs from your past, until this very moment.

Test out your own scientific mind and consider new possibilities. Push past the fear of the unknown and take a deep dive with me into the possibilities, which turned into probabilities over time, and have now been proven with exact science to, in fact be truth – even though they challenge the control of our previous assumptions and beliefs.

Let go of the need to control and learn how to tap into the creative potential that surrounds us.

The Art of Feeling Better is a finely orchestrated blend of knowledge, wisdom and focused action, starting with the letting go of all you have ever known, and all that has held you back up to this point.

Chapter 8: Using the Force

On my crazy journey so far, my intuition has led me in many strange directions, but always with the exact outcome that was needed at that time. That's the funny thing about life you see, It's simply a series of experiences collected into a finite measure of time. So the more experiences, both pleasant and unpleasant, that you can have in your life, the better.

It's all a matter of perspective. For example, ten years ago, when I would experience what I would call a 'bad' series of events, I would constantly ask myself 'Why me?' and 'Why do these things always happen to me? I'm a good person aren't I? I don't deserve this!' – when in actual fact, these events turned out to be amazing lessons and opportunities for growth that I am now extremely grateful for. (Obviously if you had told me that at the time I would most likely have said a bad word and ignored you).

The irony of Human existence is that, although the reality of life is that we are here to evolve and grow, we don't feel that we can do this without a certain level of perceived 'hardship' and 'struggle'.

We have lost touch with our truth so much that our emotional barometers are in terrible states of neglect and disrepair. It feels as though we are sabotaged at every turn, when in reality we have simply lost touch with our ancient wisdom.

Our egos fiercely fight to preserve the illusion of being separate, which is the greatest irony of all – as once we learn to embrace our connection, we can rise above the competition and conflict and into a much better space.

By looking inward and learning more about ancient wisdom teachings, blended with modern day emotional intelligence and psychology, I am learning how to flip the master switch in order to stay in the zone of 'creation and development' as much as I possibly can, even when the odds seem to be stacked against me and there are some pretty unpleasant feelings at play. It's taken a lot of research, development and work to get to this point in my own life, and unfortunately, there isn't a magic bullet solution that I can give to you to get you to the same place, as it's so personal for each unique, beautiful point of consciousness dressed up in a biological suit of armor.

What I can do however, is carefully place what I feel to be the most valuable and actionable pieces of information and parts of the puzzle that have worked for me, into a straightforward blueprint of learning, development and action which is exactly what Mindset Mojo is.

Before writing this book, I spent a couple of years putting together bitesize courses in some of the more physical and practical elements, running workshops, webinars and online courses for those who had recognized the need for change and were looking for some answers. I felt that if I could help people with some practical takeaway tools and resources then they would be able to get a head start and jump start the process of rewriting the end of their stories, just like I had done.

During this process I worked with a great many people, from different backgrounds, various ages, lifestyles, careers and passions, with a real difficulty in nailing down my demographic, as basically anyone with a brain and a heart could potentially do with some help in one area or another.

What I soon discovered was that people were starting to wake up to the fact that there was an unfulfilled need in them, that their mental or physical health, relationships or career paths, were somehow off kilter and needed a shunt (sometimes a mini nudge and sometimes a huge shove)

The forward-facing practical strategies, planning tools, templates, and even the meditations and mindfulness exercises, worked incredibly well, and brought people to a different place, however in many cases there was still something missing. Something that acted like a bungee rope and dragged people straight back down to the bottom of the mountain that they had just climbed. And it only needed to be a small, seemingly insignificant trigger in many cases.

This fascinated me. The fact that we all (myself included) have a saboteur living in our minds, that will try every sneaky trick in the book to allow us to get so far, with a false sense of security, and then at the prime moment, knock us off our perches and then proceed to kick us while we're down.

I also noticed that some people had different manifestations of this, from making amazing progress and then entering into an obviously toxic relationship which was clearly going to undo all of their hard work and take them to an even worse place before, to the person who grafts and grafts day and night working towards a brilliantly constructed SMART goal, only to flake out in some way just as they were reaching the point of smashing through their past limitations.

What's that all about? Why would we go to such lengths to make changes in our lives and then just when we are about to reach the very thing we have set the intent, planned the goals and taken all of the crucial steps towards, do we subconsciously find a way of swiping the rug out from under our own feet? It truly baffled me, and I had 'watched' myself doing it time and time again.

Just as I was pondering these very things, I began to notice a compulsion to start to research in areas that I had previously had no interest in (or assumed were far too academic for me, a lowly creative person, a 'Makeup girl' no less!)

Over the weeks and months, new subject matter would spring across my horizon, from Non-Linear Dynamics, Chaos Theory, and Advanced Quantum Theory, to ancient Hopi teachings and Shamanic Plant Medicine wisdom.

By now I had learned to never question my instincts, and that everything I had a 'feeling' towards should be investigated and a level of trust in the unknown should be employed at all times. So off I went, reading book after book and making detailed notes as things hit me, and I spotted links from one discipline to another. The whole process was absolutely enlightening, on so may levels. I began to feel my level of consciousness elevating alongside my intellectual capacity, and became excited about the implications of some of the things that I was discovering for myself.

After trying and testing out theories in my own life, that level of excitement and interest grew and grew, particularly as my scientific, logic, left brain needs were being met and marrying beautifully with my right brain, creative, visionary and intuitive side. If I could work on developing both of these areas, what would that mean for me? What would I be able to achieve? Suddenly an infinite sea of possibilities opened up for me.

So I got to work doing all of the inner stuff I had neglected to do until that point, studiously writing down and journaling all of the details as I went, evaluating what worked, what didn't, and what areas I wanted to research further.

I knew as I was going through the process that my notes would be the blueprint for a book, and some educational material to be able to help others who were on the same path. And so every bizarre coincidence, every curveball, every strange new element that seemed to get thrown into the mix, I didn't question, I just ran with, trusting that I had set the intention to find my true path and create opportunities to help others, and was walking the talk, so everything that came up would be a lesson on my journey. Either a green flag to keep moving forward or a red flag to pause, reflect and evaluate.

Nothing that I have experienced during this journey has been 'wrong' or 'wasted time'. My mind has become far more scientific in its approach, focused on the process of discovery rather than the end result of being right. When you can flip to panoramic in this way and view the bigger picture, ego starts to become less and less of a focus, you stop being afraid of failure, and you start getting excited about possibility.

Now the title of this chapter doesn't really give much away. You may have thought I was about to share some Star Wars insights with you – well you would be wrong.

One of the best books that I have ever read, that really gave me a huge shift in perception and perspective was yet another intuitive event, as I was listening to a broadcast from a keynote speaker over in America, talking about energy psychotherapy and holistic healing modalities. Another doctor who had stepped out of the ER room and begun the search for a more person centered, healing based medicine as opposed to the trauma based, last resort field medicine that he had been taught as the 'correct' modus operandi.

He briefly mentioned getting some vital information some years before from a book called 'Power vs Force' by David R. Hawkins, M.D., Ph.D, which had transformed the way in which he looked at Medicine.

He might as well have screamed the title of the book at me and posted it up as a slide in flashing lights (he didn't, he just briefly mentioned it in passing), as it immediately registered and resonated with me as something I needed to get my hands on and read right away.

By the power of Amazon Prime, it arrived on my doorstep the following day, and I quickly became engrossed, not putting it down until I had read it cover to cover and made detailed notes.

The contents of the book were a revelation to me. Confirming the thoughts that had flitted across my mind ever since I was a child. Experiencing a lifetime full of sensitivities and intuitive experiences, knowing that there was something deeper at work, something that had not yet been formally discovered or measured by modern science, but had been with us since the beginning of time, recorded by ancient civilisations, but squashed and buried by the forces of ego, corruption, tyranny and greed.

I had finally found a logical, science based, tried and tested (successfully for 25 years) explanation of all of the things I had come across during my life and my work in terms of subtle energy, and it's not so subtle effects.

As I turned the pages it was as though the metaphorical lightbulb was going off above my head, and the feeling that spread through me was one of understanding, comfort, peace, and above all truth. Real truth that resonated with every part of my being. For me, this was the missing puzzle piece that explained it all, and would help me not only to heal myself, but to work towards finding new ways to heal others.

The basic findings in the 25 years of study by Dr Hawkins, relates to everything we have discussed in this book, drawing the threads in nicely to a perfectly simple conclusion.

Using a method called 'Kinesiology' which you may or may not have heard of, it is possible to use 'muscle testing' to determine truth, bypassing the conscious mind that has all of the beLIEf's, stories and ego protection strategies in place, and straight to the sub or higher consciousness, which we now know scientifically is all connected together in that giant quantum field.

The space that we can not see, hear, smell, tease or touch, yet is all around us, listening in with it's infinite intelligence, in the spaces between things, even the spaces between our trillions of cells.

In fact, even the spaces between the cell membrane and cell nucleus. The 'matter' that we can physically measure is so teeny tiny compared to the field of subtle energy in between that we really need to shift our focus from the former to the latter.

By connecting straight in with our true selves that operate from elevated consciousness, we are able to immediately discern truth from lies, and what is more, we can actually calibrate and measure distinct 'levels' of vibrational frequency which match certain emotions and behaviours. HOW AWESOME IS THAT.

Every other scientist and medical professional that I have mentioned so far, alludes to the same thing within their work, regardless of their discipline or personal beliefs.

 It's all about the realm of the invisible, subtle energy field that surrounds us.

So let's talk a little more about this invisible vibrational frequency that we are only just starting to be able to prove scientifically, yet has always been with us, and taught in ancient mystery schools and handed down for generations through indigenous tribal teachings.

Those of you who are aware of this phenomenon, will already understand the process of 'tuning in', as we do with healing modalities such as Reiki.

We 'tap in' to a source of energy that is a different 'vibration' and allow it to flow through us in order to direct it into and around other people.

Now this has been the subject of skepticism, ignorance and ridicule for as long as I can remember, as we can not see this magical invisible force, so how can it possibly be true?! More quackery and trickery.

Not at all. In fact our ancestors and indigenous tribes from around the world have been fully aware of this and in fact used it, wrote about it, and handed down this wisdom generation upon generation, from medicine men and women dating back thousands of years.

The sadness is that these arts have been largely squashed, shunned and forgotten, but we seem to be starting a global shift towards remembering and retraining at this point in time.

If you consider for a moment the photonic spectrum of light. There is a huge variation from ultraviolet to x-ray and everything in between. We humans are only able to see a very small sliver of this in the form of the rainbow colours that are visible to our eyes. This very small spectrum of light and all of the fractals within allow us to 'see' things.

But that doesn't mean that ultraviolet and x-ray doesn't exist, in fact thanks to modern technology we are finally able to prove that it DOES, even though we can't experience it with any of our incredibly dull senses. We can explain the basics of how a TV or a mobile phone works, for example, without being able to experience first hand the energy source that makes it possible.

Our new sciences are now uncovering the great secrets of all of the invisible stuff that surrounds us – the 'space' in between things.

Known in the Science community as the 'Zero Point Field', this 'active space' is absolutely alive with vibrational energy, and is actually the field that surrounds everything in the universe, holding immense creative power, right there waiting for us to tap in to.

It's like water to a fish. The fish is oblivious to the fact that it is surrounded by water, it just lives in it, minding its own business. The Zero Point Field is to us what water is to the fish. We are literally swimming in it but we don't know it's there.

Think about batteries. All kinds of batteries, from car batteries to the AA's we put in our gadgets. Where does the energy inside a battery come from? It's harnessed from the elements in the atmosphere and stored in containers that can then be sold. But we have unlimited access to that very energy field ourselves, as Nikola Tesla was so close to showing us!

We now know that everything, everywhere is actually a 'vibration' – some things much denser and slower, which make up varying forms of physical matter, and other things vibrating at incredible frequencies, which we can not possibly pick up with our 5 senses alone. This doesn't stop them from being real and right there in front of us.

How arrogant of us to assume that only things that are picked up with our humble 5 senses are real. Or that we are the most superior and intelligent species ever to inhabit our planet. That what we can see, feel and experience through these senses is everything there is to experience, and there can be nothing more.

In order to explain the best way I can, let's return to Dr David Hawkins and his discovery that Kinesiology, or 'Muscle Testing' was a practical way to tap in to our higher selves - the 'Soul' part of us that is connected in to the zero point field and all of the knowledge and power that exists there.

I am going to simplify this greatly for the purposes of giving a general overview within the context of this book, but I strongly suggest, as many great scientists and leaders have done and had their work and discoveries greatly influenced, that you give 'Power vs Force' a good read and find out for yourself the secret weapon that we have at our disposal.

Dr Hawkins findings from all of his years of research provide a clear blueprint, detailing a scale or 'Map of Consciousness' (shown on page 85), which shows the level of energy vibration of each world view, emotion and process that we experience as human beings.

Now that we understand a little more the infinite connection between every living thing on an energetic level, it becomes easy to see how the vibrational level of one being can have a profound effect on that of another, and entire communities operating at a certain energetic vibrational frequency can have massive and far reaching implications – be that good or bad.

It's no far stretch then, when we think of the evidence in the heart-brain coherence chapter, that our own frequency output can affect not only ourselves, but other things too. The greatest evidence of this is the documented spike in the Schumann Resonance (the Earth's recorded electro-magnetic field) on September 11th 2001.

At around 9.15am, the time it took for the worlds media to spread the news of the first plane hitting the North Tower across the planet, everyone on earth had the same compassionate heart response. This actually registered as a spike in the planet's own field.

Similarly, there have been many documented cases where mass meditation had a knock-on effect of lowering emergency room cases and reducing instances of violent crime.

This all ties in with our individual 'vibrational frequencies' having a ripple effect on the whole, collective vibe, but more excitingly, the evidence that the power of higher emotions of compassion and love are far greater than the lower emotions of hate and anger, as only a small percentage of the population need to engage in the former, for the latter to also be raised up.

Have you ever been around someone who has literally drained you of every ounce of energy you have? Well that's exactly what they have done, usually unintentionally. I call them energy vampires or mood hoovers.

If you are one of the minority of people who are naturally vibrating at a higher level, either through mindfully elevating your consciousness, or you just happen to be vibing high naturally (I have found to be both in my life), then you will automatically be a magnet for others who are naturally operating at a lower level, usually through their life experiences, programmed beliefs and negative behaviour patterns.

You may have experienced the opposite in your life, coming across a person who seems to radiate energy, lifting you up and making you feel better just by being in their presence. That's a natural reaction to your need to try and evolve and elevate, your subconscious nudging you that this is the way to feel. The trouble is that this method of push-pull, accidentally stealing, manipulating and leaking energy left right and centre, is always in the 'ego' state of fighting and competing, when we have an abundance of the stuff available to us to tap into at any time.

If we get out of our own way, let our subconscious and unconscious mind take the driving seat and connect in, imagine the implications here if we can collectively educate, inspire and provide people with the tools they need to be able to shift gears.

Dr Hawkins found that any vibration below the level of 200 was below the critical point of shifting to positive experiences from elevated frequencies. States such as shame, guilt, apathy, grief, fear, desire, anger, and pride keep us operating below 200, where we sit firmly in a state of individual and collective conflict, competition and negativity. Whereas love, joy, peace, compassion and gratitude (the defining principles of Mindfulness and Meditation practices) elevate way above 200 and lead us out of that darkness.

The understanding that even when a few operate at these elevated frequencies, the power is to strong that it offsets and brings balance, even when the majority is operating at below 200 (which we can see right now at this time in history).

There has been documented evidence that if 1% of the world's population can elevate their energetic resonance enough, it will shift the balance of the entire planet. This gives me great hope for the future. We also know from Sociology studies that a critical mass of 25% positive intent and action within a community is needed to create social change, so we aren't looking to get everyone on the same page here (although how amazing would that be!)

What is needed right now, is enough elevated consciousness through the people who are feeling the pull, to boost and raise the collective. After all *'We rise by lifting others'* – *Robert Ingersoll.*

The bad news is that only 15% of the population of the planet were vibrating above 200 (at the time of his writing the book in 2014).

He talks about the fact that *"injury to our spiritual eye has resulted in a dimness of moral vision and blindness to truth"*, which keeps 85% of the population hovering below 200.

The good news is that, while we work towards a collective healing of spiritual blindness, the 15% who resonate above that critical mass point have the power to affect and offset huge numbers of people operating below. In fact, one person resonating at 400 offsets 40,000 operating below. One person at 500 is equal to 750,000. One person at 600 Is equal to 10 million, and one person at 700 is equal to 70 million people. So you can see the importance and urgency right now to help raise as many people as possible above 200 so that we can shift back out of this global funk we are stuck in.

Now I'm sure you picked up this book out of interest, with the cool title and interesting cover. Some of you will have been on your self-discovery journey for some time, while others are just starting out on the road to try and fight their way out of anxiety and depression, that feeling of being completely lost and out of control.

There is a reason you've found this book right now.

Just like I found all of the books at strange coincidental times as I was working towards my vision.

If you are able to suspend your previous assumptions just for now. Stick them in a box somewhere and just believe in the possibility of something more, something available to you right now. With a little focus, inner work and practice, you too can be part of that small percentage that creates the change that we all so badly need.

If you have been experiencing the lower emotional states mentioned above, then you will have been resonating somewhere between 0-175 (most likely around the 50-100 mark), so we need to get you up to the critical mass point of 200, and then lift you higher and higher until you tap into the space of peace, love, compassion and gratitude. Now that might seem like a major stretch right now, but trust me, with baby steps and a little faith anything is possible.

If you are too mind-blown by this new revelation, one of the continued experiments by Dr Hawkins is a brilliant way to evidence the accuracy of Kinesiology as a method of testing higher truth and calibrating frequencies.

On many, many occasions since the early 90's, one of the experiments was to have a tester and a subject with no prior knowledge of the experiment, and a big pile of books.

The format for testing anything at all is to have one person (the subject) holding an arm out straight and another person (the tester) asking a very specific question whilst putting pressure on their arm. If the arm is easily moved then you have a 'false' reading, and if the arm resists the pressure and stays true it is a 'true' reading. Sounds simple? It is, However the set up and questioning needs to be calibrated the right way so have a read of the book if you are looking to test the theory yourself.

Back to the pile of books. The blind test, which has been successful every single time, is for the tester to hold out a book and ask the subject if the book is true. If the arm stays strong then the book goes into the 'true' pile, and if it goes weak, then the book is placed in the 'false' pile.

At the end of the test, the experiment without fail leaves two distinct piles. One containing non-fiction books and one containing fictional stories. The tester nor the subject study the books or read the titles before or during the experiment.

So then the higher consciousness immediately 'knows' fact from fiction, truth from lies. Just imagine if we could find a way to use this in every area of life. Politics would look an awful lot different – but then again, that's the reason such methods as Kinesiology have been thrown in the 'quackery' pile along with all of the other truly healing modalities. It would help us restore balance and peace far too easily!

So let's bring it back to what this means for us in terms of Mindset Mojo and the journey to feeling better.

There is likely a war going on in your internal landscape right now, with chatter in your mind along the lines of 'this can't possibly be real' or 'I though this was a self-help book, not a new age manual or a science thesis' - or maybe even the internal niggle that it's way too scary to come to a place where you have the ultimate control over your own life? That healing might just be possible for you, and the constructs, beliefs and labels that make up your identity and comfort zone might be challenged in some way.

Hang in there and keep the faith. You've got this. The next steps for you are coming right up and the puzzle pieces will all fall into place. The worst that can happen is that you can finally get some relief for what has been troubling you for so long. The best is that you might just break free of the traps you've been stuck in and create a whole new reality for yourself, truly rewriting the end of your story on your terms.

What have you got to lose?

My biggest wish for you is that you are free. Free from what binds you and holds you back. Free from the emotional imprints of your past. Free to soar to new heights and experience new elevated emotions of love, peace, joy, compassion and gratitude and find your true purpose and the path that will lead you there.

Take a look at Dr Hawkins 'Map of Consciousness', and just have a think about where you might currently sit most of the time.

We all rise and fall at different times, experiencing joy in certain situations and fear or anger in others, but there will be a specific state that you calibrate in for the majority of your time. Where you sit on this scale will make up your own unique energetic frequency that you unconsciously put out into the world. Just think about what you are attracting back to yourself the majority of the time if you are stuck somewhere below 200.

I have spent a great deal of time since reading Power vs Force working on my own emotional state and trying to keep out of the lower vibes. It's not easy to 'rise above' and feel compassion, love or gratitude towards someone when they have done something to make you angry I can tell you, and we are all human, and will naturally drop from time to time.

The magic, when you start to learn this is something quite extraordinary. Not only do you feel so much better yourself, and generate happy hormones to flood your system rather than damaging ones, but the other person seems to be positively affected as well, and the knock on effect ripples out to everyone around you (just as it does when you are furious or sad)

As a species, we are bound to processes that have been constructed to keep us in survival mode. We have to operate within models that keep us locked in old restricting paradigms.
et all we need is a shift in mindset and a resulting shift in consciousness which will allow us to move into a creation space, elevating ourselves into a higher vibrational frequency, using the zero point field, which is limitless and at our 24 hour disposal.

Map of Consciousness
Developed by David R. Hawkins

The Map of Consciousness is based on a logarithmic
scale that spans from 0 to 1000.

Name of Level	Energetic "Frequency"	Associated Emotional State	View of Life
Enlightenment	700–1000	Ineffable	Is
Peace	600	Bliss	Perfect
Joy	540	Serenity	Complete
Love	500	Reverence	Benign
Reason	400	Understanding	Meaningful
Acceptance	350	Forgiveness	Harmonious
Willingness	310	Optimism	Hopeful
Neutrality	250	Trust	Satisfactory
Courage	200	Affirmation	Feasible
Pride	175	Scorn	Demanding
Anger	150	Hate	Antagonistic
Desire	125	Craving	Disappointing
Fear	100	Anxiety	Frightening
Grief	75	Regret	Tragic
Apathy	50	Despair	Hopeless
Guilt	30	Blame	Evil
Shame	20	Humiliation	Miserable

Brain training and neuroplasticity is the name of the game whichever way we look at it.

The overwhelming evidence, from multiple sources, both scientific and spiritual, points us in the direction of learning to master our emotions, work with our subtle energy field, connect our conscious and subconscious minds together, and harness our true power.

So let's recap on what we have learned so far, before we move on to some real, practical action steps to move us forward to our brand new futures.

We know that the conscious part of the mind that we are aware of, makes up around 5%, and our subconscious/unconscious mind that we are unaware of makes up 95%.

We know that we are presented with millions of bits of data per second through our senses, and our subconscious mind rapidly and automatically chooses the parts that it thinks are best for survival.

Our subconscious mind then gives us indicators in the forms of feelings, sensations and emotions which are either pleasant or unpleasant in order to guide us.

We know that our 'selves' are also our 'ego' and responsible for looking after the being that we know as 'me'. We hold our own energy frequency, or energy attractor pattern which is basically an electro-magnetic field. We also know that there is a much larger energy attractor pattern in the form of unseen waves that surround the planet (and fill the universe), that we can think of as 'universal consciousness' and this is how we are all connected.

We now know that energy attractor fields that calibrate below 200 are considered to be 'negative' and concerning the 'ego' or 'self' which results in conflict and competition, whereas the higher frequencies above 200 resonate to the higher levels of consciousness and connect us with our 'true' selves and result in unity, collaboration and cooperation and more positive outcomes.

We know that our thoughts are how we connect with the higher levels of consciousness, and every thought we connect in from the waves of possibility, then collapses into particle form and shows up as matter, and our 'reality'. It is in this way that we attract recurring people and situations and stay stuck in the negative if we hold that attractor pattern and do not change our thoughts.

We can prove that our psychology affects our biology and that thoughts connect the subconscious with the conscious mind by thinking about lemons.

Here are some exciting examples from Dr Hawkins book that show us how it is possible to elevate from a low energy field, and rise up using the power of thought to connect your conscious and subconscious minds together, to attract new levels, manifest new experiences, free yourself from the traps you have held yourself in, and rewrite the end of your story.

- *If hopelessness (calibrating at 50) can come to wanting something better (desire 125), and then use the energy of anger (150) to develop pride (175) then the next small step is the quantum leap to courage (200) which is the critical response point to get you to positive consciousness. This then has a ripple effect on your life as an individual, but also the rest of humanity by raising the collective level.*

Mindset Mojo exists to help as many people as possible to understand their true potential, regardless of where they have started from or what they have been through, and coach and support people to find their courage. (then give them a gentle nudge over the line to love, compassion and gratitude)

The toughest part of this journey is getting to the point where we can transcend the role of victim. Believe me, once you do this, nobody and nothing has any power over you.

So from this point on it's not about what happens to us, it's about how we react that makes the whole world of difference.

One crucial point to mention here is that whenever force (below 200) meets power (above 200) – Power will always defeat Force. Think about that the next time you are about to react to something and keep that vibe high.

"All levels below 200 are destructive to life in both the individual and society at large. Above 200 are constructive expressions of power" – David Hawkins, M.D, Ph.D

200 is the decisive level from falsehood to truth and from ego to unity. We just need to understand this and work with it.

Let's think about Power vs force in terms of physical health and medicine.

Conditions such as high blood pressure are said to result from an energy attractor field that is based on anger, hostility and repression, so when the symptom on it's own is treated, the context stays the same, so the underlying problem is always there. Healing however, would take away the *context* so that the energy field was elevated away from anger, hostility and repression and the thoughts and events in the persons life altered. With the new context – high blood pressure CAN NOT EXIST, so is removed from the persons life.

We can unconsciously choose anabolic (life sustaining) endorphins through our higher thought patterns, or catabolic (life limiting) stress hormones with every thought we have – both consciously and subconsciously)

It's no secret that type A personalities often succumb to heart disease, and suppressed anger leads to hypertension and stroke.

There are countless accounts as we have mentioned before of spontaneous remission from all kinds of health conditions, and it is ALWAYS attributed to a change of attitude, thoughts and thus context. Patients that completely change their context and shift their consciousness to an elevated level seem to 'magically' cure their symptoms.

Dr Hawkins put it very elegantly when he said *"The invisible universe of thought and attitude becomes visible as a consequence of body's habitual response"*

He then goes on to tell us that *"Our beliefs and attitudes associate with the specific energy attractor patterns that either correspond to power or weakness. This gives us our perception of the world, creating events to trigger specific emotions. This in turn is connected with various subtle energy pathways called 'meridians' which in turn connect with all of the organs"* – which we know about from ancient eastern medicine along with our evidence from new science.

We have seen so far with just a few of the leading professionals who have dedicated their lives to researching this subject, that spontaneous recovery from disease is possible when a shift in consciousness is present. Put in Dr Hawkins terms, the old attractor patterns that result in the pathology process no longer dominate.

The implications here are exciting and mind-blowing in equal proportions. With the advances in new views, beliefs, technology and intelligence, many health professionals are stepping into the new paradigm of person-centered medicine. What was once viewed as 'hoaxes' 'hallucinations' and 'quackery' are now provable by science and the realisation is that our health system is misaligned with lower energy attractor patterns of force, plastering over the cracks that appear on scans and x-rays, long after disease is well underway.

When physicians start to work from a higher paradigm, connecting with the higher energy attractor patterns, taking time to understand the persons whole story and context and valuing non-traditional modalities in their therapeutic approaches, then we can really start to heal. The term 'holistic practitioner' has always been seen as 'less than', ever since John D Rockerfella outlawed any other modality than the drugs and surgeries cause and effect model of his new Med-Schools. The truth, as we see in 'Power Vs Force' needs no defense, and as we can see right now, although the intellect (ego) is easily fooled, the heart (higher connected consciousness) knows the truth.

Now, let me talk about many of the people who we assume are 'winning' at life and where they calibrate.

When we elevate a bit and feel like we've cracked it, we need to be mindful that we've actually got ourselves above 200 and aren't just hovering around the level of Pride at 175. At this level of consciousness it's very easy to feel like you've smashed it, only to be knocked off your perch and have the rug pulled out from under you, ending up right back where you were and back into victimhood and much lower levels.

An inflated ego is vulnerable to attack and you can fall super easy if you're not committed to raising your vibe to a place of unity, compassion and love for both self AND others. That's the magic key.

I have been here so many times, feeling like I'm winning, only to be shoved back down to the bottom of the pit where I can safely reinforce that negative belief that I don't deserve it, am not good enough, and it always happens to me yada yada yada. The context is still the same. My self-belief and beliefs about the world have not changed. I have just managed to claw my way up to a place where I've achieved a little win – but my subconscious is right there waiting to keep me in check as it knows we're not really there yet.

You will notice that TRULY successful people aren't phased by knock backs. They view them as stepping-stones to greater things. Learning opportunities that they can genuinely be grateful for. The majority of the population don't think like this and revert straight back to victimhood, way down the consciousness ladder.

Once we have jumped above the 200 point, and are accessing elevated emotions like trust, forgiveness, peace, compassion, joy and gratitude it's really hard for anything to stand in our way to success. The small wins feel amazing and we are grateful for the lessons along the way. We breeze through set-backs and blast through obstacles because we 'know' we are on the right path. We are aligned with our truth, and working with both parts of our minds, in coherence with our hearts, and connected in with source energy with a ton of power at our disposal.

Think about the point of becoming 'empowered' at 200. Where exploration, determination, creativity, challenge, excitement and the willingness to try new things come into play. That special place of being able to cope with new opportunities, to learn and develop new skills, to face your fears and grow.

To be in that place of 'learning to surf' – riding the waves and being ok with disappointments. Achieving that inner confidence and becoming non-judgemental. Recognising the power of selfnessness vs the force of self-interest. Finding your true power to serve yourself and others, rather than using self-serving force.

Most importantly we realise that we are connected to something bigger than ourselves. We recognize the importance of others and value community, collaboration and cooperation above competition and conflict.

So what, I hear you ask, after that incredibly deep and brain-bending chapter, do I do to use all of this information and change my life?

I'm glad you asked.

Keep reading and I'll take you further down the path, to some real, practical take away tools that you can start to use right away to raise your vibe.

Chapter 9: Rewriting your Story

"Merely observing the mind raises our level of consciousness"
- Dr David Hawkins

The good news, after all of the things that you have learned so far, is that the 'Art of Feeling Better' is simply a skill that you can learn, practice, and develop. Sometimes you just need to get out of your own way.

By learning about how your brain works, how your mind and body connect, and the added knowledge that you have the power to connect into a field of consciousness that you didn't even know was there to make profound changes in your life, is automatically going to raise your vibration up to excitement and hope for the future, so you're shifting simply by reading this book and absorbing the words,

Starting right now, this new insight should be enough to give you a little hope for the future, and a little faith that new things are possible for you.

The best part of the process starts here, when you can start to build on all of this new knowledge and put it all to the test.

We learned in chapter 1, all about you. What makes you tick and what pushes your buttons. In chapter 2 we looked at how your sympathetic nervous system works, in modern times keeping us locked in what we now know of as lower energy attractor patterns.

In chapter 3 we looked at our triggers and what kind of thoughts really stress us out and are holding us back. We also looked at some initial ways to push through our limiting thoughts that make us anxious, and take action regardless (which we now know of as the level of courage which will elevate us to new frequency vibes)

Chapter 4 taught us about the importance of emotional intelligence and we learned how Lobsters grow by recognizing uncomfortable sensations as red flags, showing us the way to learn, develop and evolve. We also looked at how we don't do this in modern, western society, but stay trapped in a prison of running away from our feelings instead.

We looked at the Mind-Body connection in chapter 5, learning that we are more than just our physical selves. That there is much more out there in terms of subtle energy fields that have a huge effect on us without us even realizing it. We proved how our psychology does in fact become our biology by thinking about lemons!

Chapter 6 saw us discovering heart-brain coherence and the missing puzzle piece of connecting the two parts of ourselves together to blend logic and reasoning with our internal truth, and higher consciousness in order to heal ourselves and finally free us from our prisons and set us on our true path.

In chapter 7 we moved on for a whistlestop tour of the subject of control. We looked at our comfort zones being prisons and found out what things we need to let go of in order to start moving forward.

With all of the new knowledge and the exercises in the first seven chapters I then threw you in with a deep dive to discover the secrets of the subtle energy system we had discovered earlier, with some solid scientific evidence into its qualities, our relationship to it, and behaviours as a result of it. We looked at how we are able to empower ourselves and raise our energetic attractor pattern or 'vibration' to match the universal pattern of the good stuff such as love, peace, compassion and gratitude, and that would then attract those sorts of experiences into our lives.

So we have a clear path of knowledge at this point, of how we really can re-write the rest of our story, no matter where we are right now or where we have come from. We simply need to start to behave like the lobster and learn to recognize our uncomfortable sensations, feelings and emotions as real blessings, pointing us in the right direction and helping us out of the lower energy attractor patterns and into the spaces that feel good – usually places of love, compassion, joy, peace and gratitude which are of course way above 200.

If we now know that we are stuck in anger the majority of the time and we need to get ourselves up higher, we need to recognize what it is that makes us angry. Where has it come from? What do we need to do to let it go? What actions can we take to turn that anger into pride and then courage to step out of that particular trap?

The final two chapters include some of the action steps from my Mindset Mojo 'life laundry' and 'finding your feet' courses – specifically designed to give you a blueprint and a formula to follow in order to climb that ladder from wherever you are starting from, to the courage of 200 and beyond.

There are many more activities that you can engage in to do this so please dive in and do some research – read some of the suggested materials and keep your journey moving forward by experimenting and finding new things that work for you, that you can then pass on to others.

For me, the logical next step towards rewriting your story is to find out what it is that may be holding you in the lower attractor patterns.

The following activity, I found incredibly hard to do when I first did it, as it meant admitting to myself what was really going on. All of the things about myself that my subconscious knew were bringing me trouble and had tried countless times to give me nudges of uncomfortable feelings about, but my conscious intellectual ego who always thinks its far superior and right, masked over and stored away somewhere – out of sight out of mind.

I am forever grateful for this exercise and have used it in countless seminars and workshops, always with the same consciousness shifting results.

You'll find a template on the next page, of a mask that you can draw out twice onto some paper (Yep this one is a two-part task and they are both as important as each other)

I'd like to know, what masks do you wear? What roles do you play? What do you let people see? What's hidden on the inside? I'd like you to fill the first one in with some words, and I want it to represent what you show to the world. What do people see when they look at you? What do you let people see? What do you show on the front?

When you've done that, I'd like you to do the second one but, this time, the inside. What do you hide away? What is it that you don't let people see?

This exercise is really important because it digs so much deeper and it lets us see all of the things are that you're hiding away so that we can have a look at why that might be. The trick is to be able to get aligned, so that what you're projecting out on the front is the real you, what actually makes you happy, and you don't have to feel that fear anymore, of what people are going to think or say, or how people are going to judge you. You just show them the real you and the right people will come along.

We can then use this to work out the people, events and situations that keep us held in the places of fear, anger, sadness, envy and all of the lower emotions that keep us trapped.

We can use this 'lobster' knowledge to start to think about ways to elevate above this. Maybe we can let a situation from our past go and forgive someone? Perhaps we need to remove toxic people and create better boundaries? Maybe it's finally time to forgive ourselves for something from our past and move on?

Whatever comes up for you, just sit with it for a while, feel the feelings and process any emotions that come up that you might have buried up to this point. See what you can let go of, and what you can note down that needs some additional work.

Now that we are starting to engage in your 'shadow work' - that is, illuminating the things that have been hidden in the darkness for so long, we can really make some breakthroughs with connecting your conscious and subconscious mind. We know now that the intellect can be fooled, but the heart knows the truth, so why don't you revisit the heart-brain coherence meditation in chapter 6, and ask yourself the question that is now much more relevant than before –

'what do I need to let go of in order to move forward?'.
See what comes up now and write it down.

Then follow up with the question –
'what do I need to do (or do more of) in order to move forward on my true path?'

When you start to have a clearer picture and the revelations come through, the realization of where you've been stuck all this time, and attach that to an emotion on the map of consciousness scale, you can see where you sit and plan out your journey from there.

If you've been sitting with humiliation, blame, despair, anxiety, hatred or scorn, then at least you know, and you know that there is a way out now. Whatever level you feel you're at, take a non-judgemental look at it, recognize it for what it is, a response to a collection of life experiences that you've had so far that no longer serve you and you can let go of now.

Look at how you might be able to start to climb the ladder towards courage by taking small baby steps each day, such as the exercises in this book, or thousands of other mindfulness and self-development tools out there. Remember that simply the act of observing your mind and recognizing your truth (which you are doing right now), elevates your consciousness anyway and boosts you up that ladder.

My next action step for you is to work out your 'why'.

Another important part of the jigsaw. You need to know and understand what it truly important to you in your life. If you miss this step then it's easy for you to get blown off course by the needs, wishes and intentions of everyone else, when the right path for you is just that. The right path for YOU.

It is crucially important to know what matters to you, and algin everything you do from this point with your truth.

Take a look at the list of core values here, and think about the ones that resonate with you the most. Circle or note down 5 or 10 that really feel true to you and keep those at the front of your mind whenever you make any decisions or set any intentions from this point on.

MY CORE VALUES

Acceptance, Authenticity, Achievement, Accomplishment, Adventure, Authority, Balance, Beauty, Boldness, Compassion, Clarity, Cleanliness, Commitment, Cooperation, Courage, Creativity, Courtesy, Citizenship, Determination, Dependability, Equality, Fairness, Faith, Friendship, Fun, Growth, Generosity, Gratitude, Happiness, Honesty, Humour, Honour, Joy, Kindness, Knowledge, Loyalty, Leadership, Learning, Love, Patience, Popularity, Peace, Pleasure, Passion, Perserverance, Punctuality, Respect, Recognition, Reputation, Resilience, Responsibility, Security, Self-Respect, Stability, Success, Status, Trustworthiness, Tolerance, Wealth

In order to keep that vibe building we need to get you fired up and in the zone of courage, willingness and acceptance that your life can be different, and you do have the power to change.

By thinking about things that inspire us, we generate the kind of thoughts that we have mentioned previously. Ones that calibrate at a higher frequency and make us feel good. Ones that release anabolic, or life sustaining endorphins, and make us feel as though anything were possible.

One of the ways we can do this is by focusing on what inspires us, rather than what limits us.

Use your journal to start to write down all of the things, people, places, music, movies, and events that inspire you and make you feel elevated. Revisit these on a daily basis and study them, looking for connections and ways in which you can experience them more and more. How can you make these things a constant part of your everyday life?

This exercise leads us beautifully on to my next step in re-writing your story.

What would your perfect life look like? Have you ever even dared to think about that before? Ever given yourself permission to dream?

What if you had a blank piece of paper and no limits, how would you write your life wish list?

Off you go. That's exactly what you have.

You can crack straight on with your ultimate bucket list, or you can start with a 'perfect' day scenario and build it from there.

Give yourself the permission to think and dream big, as big as you like. Nothing and nobody has the power to hold you back at this point. Only you. You just need to get out of your own way.

I challenge you to write out as much as you can, describing how your perfect life would look, from the most minute details of daily life, to the big accomplishments and achievements.

Think in terms of personal, career, and financial goals and hold nothing back. Think as big as you can.

Reinforce this by detailing your own unique gifts and skills, and how you are going to use them to help and support yourself, the people around you, and the planet. Really dig deep and uncover what your own personal superpower is. Whether it be your kindness, affinity with animals, skills with numbers, writing, music, building, designing, cooking, art, working with others, negotiating skills, being an awesome parent, teaching something to others – the list is endless, and you DO have your own unique superpower. It's time to uncover it now.

This is how we start to build you towards courage, inspiration, self-belief, confidence in your abilities. Knowing your truth.

Then anything is possible.

Chapter 10: Changing the Future

So what happens next? What's the final piece of the puzzle? Are you ready for your future?

Here's the crucial point for you, the ultimate piece of wisdom that I've been excited to share with you from the very beginning.

There is no final jigsaw piece for me to give you. It's all about you now. I can't tell you what to do next, where to go, what will make you happy and fulfilled, or what your true path is. Only you know this, and whether your conscious mind fights you on it or not, that deep wisdom and true knowing is in there somewhere, just waiting to break free.

It is my deepest intention that the words in this book, and the practical activity suggestions held within its pages have sparked something within you that has opened up new possibilities, new thoughts, feelings and emotions. My purpose in life and the path I now walk is to light the touch paper in as many people as possible, sparking the fire that will start to glow and grow, until you are lit up from the inside and radiating your truth. I want to give you the confidence and belief that you are a beautiful, unique and limitless being, capable of truly amazing things, and even if you have no idea how, where, when or even what, you now know the 'why' that will lead you out of the darkness of fear, anger, shame, guilt and envy and into the light of courage, truth, acceptance, love, and compassion.

The path in front of you is an exciting expedition to reclaim your true power, and you should grab it with both hands, taking small steps each day, like the tiny cogs in a machine that go on to turn the major wheels of change.

By expanding your mental framework from the limits of your 'personality' – that part of us that we believe makes up 'ourselves', and realizing that the elements of our personality are simply constructs that keep us trapped, we can see that this does not reflect our true selves, but the masks that we have collected through our lives so far.

Through a combination of programmed beliefs and coping strategies, we have constructed these masks, which are really just distortions created through our subconscious in an effort to protect us from perceived danger. They are simply attachments that we have formed that no longer serve us - fear reactions and negative ego coming into play.

The hero's journey from this point is to focus not just on the physical parts of us that we have been consumed with for so long, but to create balance by spending time and energy on the deeper stuff, working out where our barriers sit and how they got there in the first place.

Working on the roots and not the fruits is the goal now, and the secret key to unlocking everything else. Where have we created attachments that are really not serving us any-more? Where have we given our power away? To whom, and why?

In what ways do we resist our own progression and see our internal saboteur come out? Where do we engage in negative emotional dynamics with others?

All of these are crucial questions that you need to start giving your attention to, in order to start unblocking the things that are holding you back. Only by going back and healing our inner child can we release and let go of the old attachments that have kept us imprisoned for so long.

You may be fully aware at this point, which emotional traumas in your past may have created attachments and coping mechanism behaviour patterns, or you may be completely unaware.

There could be an emotional imprint from a time when you were 6 years old and had something exciting to share with a parent, but at that time they were preoccupied with a phone call or reading a book. At that point your 6 year old self may have programmed in that what you have to say is not important, you are not worthy of being listened to, or you are not loved. This may have had a massive impact on your subconscious thoughts, decisions and behaviours from that moment on, causing you to get stuck in a loop of behaviours that attract the same kind of experiences and people, which then reinforce those self-limiting beliefs.

You can see the pattern emerging here can't you? Such distortions can last a lifetime if we do not shine a light on them. Uncover them, acknowledge and process them, and remove them to create some space for the new stuff. This is called shadow-work, and has been THE most important part of my journey so far.

No amount of force, hard graft, and sheer will power will get you where you need to be, if that iceberg below the surface that you are unaware of, is working against you and keeping your energy vibe low.

So what next?

What are the practical next steps that the logical, physical, rational, conscious ego self needs to take in order to get where we want to go?

Is there a roadmap to life? I feel that there is. After years of searching, learning and developing, for me, I have found that we simply need to start developing our intuition – or conversations with our subconscious.

We know that we already operate primarily from our 5 physical senses, and that does help us navigate our physical world on a practical level, but it's also what keeps us locked in our prisons of distorted, limiting self-beliefs and negative ego chatter.

So developing that other, mysterious side to us that we tend to close off and ignore, needs to come into balance. Learning to use our judgement and discernment, setting healthy parameters and boundaries, are crucially important as we have already discussed. If you haven't already written anything down in your journal along these lines then I encourage you to do that as your first priority.

We can only do this, as we know, when we are aware of what makes us happy and fulfilled, what our gifts and talents are, and what we feel our purpose and path in life are.

We have already visited several times the famous quote: *'Knowledge is Power'*, but knowledge for knowledge's sake is pointless. Knowledge towards progression is key.

So I encourage you to keep on researching, studying and learning, whilst at the same time applying what you have learned to your every day life, in whichever ways feel true and right to you.

I would love to invite you to join me on one of my practical workshops or courses, to learn some of the skills and strategies that have helped me on my journey so far. There is nothing more powerful than connecting with a community of like-minded people who can inspire, support and motivate each other. After all....... We really do rise by lifting others – *(Robert Ingersoll)*.

If you're ready to take that next step then please feel free to follow the instructions at the end of this book to connect in with the Mindset Mojo resources, but if you're not in that space quite yet, then that is exactly the place in your journey that you are meant to be.

I would encourage you to read this book again and see what else you can pull out of it. Make some notes and engage in the activities – this alone will automatically increase your energy, both physical and subtle, and start you on your new path.

I have two more things that I would like to share with you before the end of this book. The first is my challenge to you to start to cultivate a brand new attitude, right now, to take forward with you for the rest of your life. An attitude of gratitude. We have learned a lot about the stress hormones we constantly release, but what about a tip to get us releasing some of the good stuff?

The first thing I'd like to teach you is how to instantly turn your sympathetic nervous system off, so that you can shut down the cortisol and adrenaline response as quickly as possible. I call it 'Balloon Breathing' or 'Anchor Breathing'.

It's a simple trick, using the evidence that by making your exhale at least twice as long as your inhale, you can switch your fight or flight response off.

I do this by imagining that I have to inflate a large balloon under my ribs as quickly as possible, so I take a huge breath in as if I were about to hold my breath. Then I hold for a couple of seconds (if I can), before releasing as slowly as I possibly can, as though I were blowing a balloon up normally, but through a tight opening. Using this visualization technique I usually find that my inhale takes about 2 seconds but I can extend my exhale to about 20, which is obviously way more than double! Try it – it works every time.

So once you have your nervous system under control, it's time to really release those happy chemicals and start to elevate our vibe on a physical level, so that we can cultivate practices that work from the top down (working on the mind to produce an effect on the body), but also from the bottom up, by working on the physical body and altering your biochemistry, so that your mind starts to play ball and follow suit.

The most potent positivity chemicals we have available to us on tap through our biochemistry are Oxytocin, Seratonin and Dopamine, and when we experience gratitude, we light all of these up at once.

Once we learn to bypass the role of victimhood and activate an attitude of gratitude, we can stimulate feelings of pleasure and contentment – even when our physical reality may be anything but.

Robert Brault famously encouraged us to *"enjoy the little things, for one day you may look back and realise that they were the big things"* – this could not be truer.

The benefits of gratitude are far reaching into all areas of our lives, if we can learn to tap into it whenever possible. From enhanced mood, greater self-awareness, and stronger inter-personal relationships, to a stronger immune system, better sleep-wake cycles and optimum blood pressure and cardiac functioning. Who doesn't want that?

Gratitude works on so many levels, and when sustained, some studies show that on the map of consciousness it calibrates at 900 on the scale shown so it's super high, making it the highest possible emotional state, so it can only help raise us, right?

Gratitude leads us to true happiness, as it helps us to realise that we are on the right path, we are making small steps and achieving wins all along the way. We should never give up hope, and just need to keep moving towards those things that we have found that we're grateful for and make us happy.

Raising our level of optimism, selflessness, empathy, self-esteem and spirituality, we can see how this truly is the most important attitude we can work on to get us where we want to go.

I realise how hard it is when you feel like you're at the bottom of the pit. So that leads us to my final task, which, teamed with an attitude of gratitude will have the most profound effect on both your external and internal life, so I would also like you to work on every day from this point on.

In order to bring together everything that you have learned in this book, pulling the threads together and actually actioning the kind of change you have been reading about, you need to look at all of the surface activities and notes you have worked on so far, and this time view them through a specific lense.

I want you to look back through the things that stress you out, the triggers and anxieties you face, the masks you wear, and the big dreams, goals and skills that you have that you've kept hidden away from the world, and ask yourself the following question that we have already visited:

"What are the barriers that are holding me back right now"

And then the second part to the question, "where did they come from" (or you could ask yourself when you can remember first feeling or experiencing them)

If you struggle with this, you can go back and do the Heart-Brain coherence meditation to get yourself into alignment with both conscious and subconscious mind, and ask again. Journal your answers.

This exercise will really dig deeper to the roots, and unearth the core of what your next step needs to be.

I can't stress highly enough that your self-talk is a symptom of the underlying problem, and once we get to the roots in this way, we can easily uncover the self-talk we give ourselves 95% of the time. Our internal chatter just below the surface is what drives us to make most of our decisions, and it is almost always negative, and created through our distorted and warped lenses from our past.

By unpicking and tracing back to it's origins, we can simply recognize, acknowledge, and release whatever it was, from the distracted parent who didn't rejoice in our macaroni necklace, to the kid at school who told us we were ugly. Whatever it was is in the past, and that's where it needs to go right now. Holding on to it does not serve you, or anybody else, in any way. It is what's keeping you operating at 'below 200' and keeping you stuck in the loop.

We need to start asking ourselves the right questions. So rather than 'why does this always happen to me?', lets start to ask 'so where has this come from, and what do I feel I need to do in order to release it?'

Once we start to come into self-awareness and realization, we are already liberating and raising our vibration, so it becomes a much more achievable step to reach the level of courage, where I have no doubt you are right now. We just need to keep you there.

Dr Theresa Bullard is a physicist who has spent the past few years following her Ph.D, uncovering the parallels between the new science she had followed as her chosen career, and the ancient mystery schools, that have always taught the very subject matter covered in this book. She very elegantly speaks of 'Spiritual Alchemy' and the process of elevating and evolving into something more.

In one of her videos, which I really love, she breaks down the process of our individual evolution into the metaphor of a caterpillar as it builds its chrysalis. Moving into a space as one particular 'self', and breaking down into complete chaos, only to rebuild into something new and improved. At surface glance the 'soupy mess' inside the chrysalis bears no resemblance to the original form, or the new one, and it's impossible to tell what will become of the creature, or how it does what it does. But the blueprint held inside it's very DNA knows exactly what it needs to do and at exactly the right time. Rebuilding cell by cell, just like it was destined to do all along in order to reach it's full potential. It doesn't have any negative self-talk holding it back. No 'what if people won't like me' or 'what if my bum looks big in my new form'. It just knows.

Once we free ourselves from these chains, and allow our deeper knowing to come through. Once we shine a light on our shadow selves and work to heal our inner child, we are able to mature spiritually, and develop into something truly amazing.

Whatever your background or beliefs, whether you pray to God or Buddha, The Universe or your own Higher-Self - the texts, teachings and findings from new science all point towards the same fundamental principles as the ancient ones. Life is about learning, experiencing and gathering knowledge in order to progress. Raising yourself to the higher realms of love and unity and practicing compassion and tolerance.

We can see by looking at many ancient texts, including the bible, that the guiding principles of not stealing, lying, hating on other people, letting ego and pride take over (all of the lower levels) have been there all along to guide us, whatever our religious or spiritual inclinations. Pointers towards living in truth, unity, higher awareness and connecting with something more have been around us for centuries – we just forget to check in with our own internal GPS system and we throw away our maps, only to get caught up in other people's dramas, story's, wants and needs.

Actively engage in your internal chatter. Monitor and influence your self-talk, and make a conscious effort to plant some positive seeds in there, and consistently do some good old pruning and weeding.

It's your time now. Time to take your power back. Find that balance between Warrior and Healer. So many of us sit at either one end of the spectrum or the other, either giving away our power and sacrificing ourselves for others, or shutting out love and ending up competitive and cruel.

The Art of Feeling Better is all about finding your own personal balance. Your own perfect version of you, and writing out your own prescription for what you need more of in your life to heal, empower and inspire you to greatness.

Your onward journey is to find your own personal keys and unlock your chains.

It really is true, that the truth shall set you free. We need to close our eyes and dream …… and open our eyes and see.

References & Recommended Reading Material

Inner Story
O'brien. T., 2015. *Inner Story. (Place of publication not identified):* Ideational

The Chimp Paradox
Peters, S., n.d. *The Chimp Paradox.*

The Biology of Belief
Lipton, B., n.d. *The Biology Of Belief.*

Power vs Force
Hawkins, D., 2014. *Power Vs. Force.* Hay House Inc.

Everything you need to know to feel good
Pert, C., 2007. *Everything You Need To Know To Feel Good.* [Place of publication not identified]: Hay House Inc.

Quantum Healing
Chopra, D., 2015. *Quantum Healing.* [Place of publication not identified]: Bantam Books.

The Secret of Perfect Living
Mangan, J., 2006. *The Secret Of Perfect Living.* West Conshohocken, Pa.: InfinityPublishing.com.

Evolve your Brain/Breaking the Habit of Being Yourself
Dispenza, J., 2009. *Evolve Your Brain.* Deerfield Beach, Fla.: Health Communications. (Breaking the Habit of Being yourself is also awesome)

I've got to get out of my own way/Growing Up
Twerski, A., n.d. *Growing Up.*

Dr Theresa Bullard
Dr Theresa Bullard. 2020. *Dr Theresa Bullard.* [online] Available at: <https://theresabullard.com/> [Accessed 4 October 2020].

Next Steps

I would love to invite you to join me on one of my short courses, challenges, webinars or coaching programmes, whichever you feel drawn to at this time.

You can find all of the information at:
https://mindset-mojo.teachable.com/p/home

or

https://www.mindsetmojo.co.uk/

Recommended Partners

I would also like to recommend some practical self-help trusted partners who are ready to help you with your onward journey through their products and services.

Take a look at the following pages and get in touch with any of my good friends that you feel drawn to connect with.

Sheila Patel
Business Coach & Mentor

My journey to freedom

Life gets better by change, not by chance

My husband had to have spinal surgery, my children were growing up and leaving home, and then the bombshell dropped that I had an aggressive form of Breast Cancer.

My world crashed.

Recovery, for me was based on a shift in mindset, realising the importance of taking control of our own health. After in depth research and a lot of scepticism I started my wellness business, promoting the benefits of using products made with pure inner leaf Aloe Vera gel.

Get in touch today to find out more and start your journey to Wellness

07746 647777   sheilspatell2@hotmail.com   fb: Sheila Patel   IG: @SheilaPatelGlobal

Printed in Poland
by Amazon Fulfillment
Poland Sp. z o.o., Wrocław

63638201R00068